The Art of the Literature, Volum

## *The Strange Case of Dr. ~~Jekyll~~*

## *Mr. Hyde*

# PERIPETEIA PRESS

Published by Peripeteia Press Ltd.

First published: January 2021

ISBN: 978-1-913577-06-3

Check out our A-level English Literature website, peripeteia.webs.com

# Contents

| | |
|---|---:|
| Introduction | 5 |
| **Chapter Commentaries** | |
| Chapter 1 | 11 |
| Chapter 2 | 19 |
| Chapter 3 | 25 |
| Chapter 4 | 30 |
| Chapter 5 | 35 |
| Chapter 6 | 40 |
| Chapter 7 | 45 |
| Chapter 8 | 49 |
| Chapter 9 | 56 |
| Chapter 10 | 61 |
| **Settings** | 63 |
| **Characters** | |
| Jekyll | 68 |
| Hyde | 72 |
| Utterson | 76 |
| Lanyon | 79 |
| Minor characters | 84 |

## Themes

Twinship and disability                           92

The gentleman question                            95

Homosexuality, clubland and secrecy              100

Father and son                                   105

Darwinism and degeneration                       109

Drugs and addiction                              113


## Glossary of terms                             117


## Recommended reading                           120


## About the authors                             121

# Introduction

## The Gothic

The Gothic is a genre that unsettles, terrifies, distorts and questions all that is believed to be normal, whilst simultaneously intriguing the reader. Although Stevenson's novella had a turbulent start, especially with his wife [Fanny Stevenson] rejecting it for being too dark, the title *The Strange Case of Dr. Jekyll and Mr. Hyde* is now embedded in popular culture, just as much as other seminal Gothic novels, such as, *Frankenstein* [1818] and *Dracula* [1897]. Why is there so much fascination with the Gothic, if it frightens and disturbs its readers? Why has the genre continued to grip readers, if it taps into the very things we would rather avoid acknowledging?

According to Jerrold Hogle, the 'longevity of Gothic fiction unquestionably stems from the way it helps us address and disguise some of the most important desires, quandaries, and sources of anxiety from the most internal to the widely social and cultural throughout the history of western culture'.[1] Through the Gothic icons of Frankenstein's creature, Dracula and Hyde, the Gothic '[raises] the possibility that all "abnormalities" we […] divorce from ourselves are a part of ourselves'.[2] As with other Gothic fiction, Stevenson's novella provides the ideal platform to negotiate anxieties that shape both our identities and the world we live in.

---

[1] Jerrold E. Hogle, 'Introduction: The Gothic in Western Culture' in *The Cambridge Companion to Gothic Fiction*, ed. by Jerrold E. Hogle, (Cambridge: Cambridge University Press, 2002), pp. 1-20 (p. 1).

[2] Hogle, p. 12.

It is no wonder that Robert Louis Stevenson's novella has and continues to make such a profound impact upon those that encounter it. The novella was published in 1886, amidst the backdrop of the *Fin-de-Siècle* and this was the ideal period for the birth *The Strange Case of Dr. Jekyll and Mr. Hyde*. As Glennis Byron points out, it was an era where 'boundaries were crumbling, the empire in decline, the comfortable middle-class family and its values threatened by forces from both within and without'.[3] Byron also states that the genre enables 'all barriers [to be] broken down and all secret spaces penetrated'.[4] Certainly, the genre's ability to access 'secret spaces' is at the core of Stevenson's novella and it really forces us to pose the question: Do we really present our real selves to the world? Or do we, like Jekyll, have secret selves?

Stevenson's novella explores a fundamental otherness that can be read, and has been read, in myriad ways. As an oblique commentary on the demonization of homosexually or as a response to the unsettling ideas of Darwin or Freud, for instance. In addition, Stevenson also taps into Victorian anxieties about science and how scientific experiments could release secrets that are, perhaps, better left alone.

Not only does *The Strange Case of Dr. Jekyll and Mr. Hyde* set out to explore late nineteenth-century anxieties, it also releases Stevenson's own inner demons. After all, his childhood was plagued by repeated sickness, which led to periods of isolation, and as such, he felt increasingly disconnected from the outer world of Edinburgh. As he

---

[3] Glennis Byron, 'Introduction' in *Dracula: New Casebooks* (Basingstoke: Macmillan, 1999), pp. 1-21 (p. 2).

[4] Byron, p. 2.

matured, he became much more aware of the repressive conventions of the New Town, leading him to feel attracted to the Old Town. Already, it is clear that the novella's central concern of a 'double existence' was inspired by Stevenson's own experiences. He was propelled to the darkness of the Old Town, as it provided an escape route from all that he despised. He craved independence and recognised that this could only be achieved through splitting his desires from the pretence of conformity.[5] Stevenson's situation parallels and reflects that of Jekyll's and all the male characters in the novella, as they strive to cover their baser, inner desires with the outwardly respectable appearance and earnest behaviour of the Victorian gentleman. However, through Jekyll's character, Stevenson clearly warns us that repression is toxic and will corrupt the soul.

Plagued by ghosts, vampires, revenants and such-like, Gothic fiction is always concerned with the enduring power of the past and the return of the repressed. Hence Hyde can be read as an earlier, less civilized version of humanity, as an atavistic self, who lives, albeit caged, even the most civilised of men, Henry Jekyll.

The earliest Gothic novels, such as Horace Walpole's *The Caste of Otranto* [1764], featured settings such as medieval castles, ruined monasteries, graveyards and dungeons in foreign locations, locations faraway in terms of both space and time from the world of their readers. Such haunted spaces may have been used by novelists to explore society's deepest fears and terrors, but there was a comforting gap between text and reader. One of major innovations in the Gothic genre that makes Stevenson's novella so compelling and disturbing is

---

[5] To discover more about Stevenson's background, an interesting account of his life is given in a BBC documentary series, 'The Birth of Horror.'

his decision to bring terror right home, into the present-day and onto

 the bustling streets of Victorian London – the urban gothic landscape.[6] This shift in setting removes the reassuring distance between readers and Gothic characters, bringing the novella's presiding concerns - degeneration, decay and hidden desires right onto the doorsteps and even into familiar, domestic spaces of its readers, uncomfortably and unsettlingly close to home.

The fact that the Gothic genre has continued to flourish since Walpole's *The Castle of Otranto* demonstrates the longevity of the genre. Why has it continued to survive the test of time? David Punter, a key scholar of the genre, notes that one of the reasons for the genre having survived is that it is 'cyclical [...] [and] re-emerges in times of cultural stress'.[7] In addition, the Gothic has mutated and spread itself widely as a genre. As one critic notes it has 'scattered its ingredients into various modes' and elements of it can be traced 'in flamboyant plays and operas, short stories, fantastic tales for magazines and newspapers',[8] as well as appearing in 'sensation novels for women,

---

[6] It is worth reading Bram Stoker's *Dracula,* as the same strategy is employed. Jonathan Harker visits Transylvania, thus entering an eastern landscape, but the threat of Count Dracula, as 'The Other' invades Victorian London.

[7] David Punter, *The Gothic,* (Oxford: Blackwell Publishers, 2004), p. 20.

[8] Hogle, p. 1.

literature for the working-class, and portions of poetry and paintings'.[9] Clearly, the influence of the Gothic genre upon the literary landscape is profound.

Unlike the early wave Gothic texts, late nineteenth-century Gothic texts responded to concerns surrounding social, internal, national decay and degeneration. As Britain's imperialist power and influence diminished, fears grew that outsiders could invade the supposedly impenetrable fortress of the Victorian world – something that Bram Stoker's *Dracula* explores through Count Dracula. Alongside this, the Gothic was also articulating the concerns that Darwin had induced through evolution, with the possibility that a species could regress down the evolutionary chain. Essentially, it was Darwin's evolutionary theories that revealed that 'human beings [are] just a species like any other [...] rather than [having a] providential design.'[10]

The genre does not stop there. Concerns about criminality hidden under respectability, concerns about disease and the potential for the primitive to infect the civilized world all became characteristic elements of Gothic fiction. Even more so, the idea of the double and the vampire returned, and were more 'potent literary myths' than ever before. Ultimately, the fin de siècle, was an era, as Glennis Byron writers, where 'boundaries were crumbling' the 'empire was in decline' and the 'comfortable middle-class family and its values' was under threat both from forces 'within and without'.

And the genre has continued to grow from strength to strength. As

---

[9] Hogle, p. 1.

[10] Kelly Hurley, 'British Gothic Fiction,' in *The Cambridge Companion to Gothic Fiction*, ed. by Jerrold E. Hogle, (Cambridge: Cambridge University Press, 2002), pp. 189-207 (p. 194).

one critic points out, the Gothic has proven that it can blend into all forms, as Gothic tropes can be traced in 'films, ghost stories, [...] women's romantic novels, television shows, romantic and satirical plays, and computerized games and music videos'.[11]

The Gothic is still very much with us, as illustrated by the work of Laura Purcell in her book *The Silent Companions* (2017), in which she reimagines and returns to many of the Gothic tropes that were first established by Walpole.

Overall, the Gothic genre is designed to terrify and frighten us so that we question our surrounding environment, and also question our sense of ourselves and our positions in society. As Glennis Byron argues, the Gothic:

> 'exposes and explores the desires, anxieties and fears that both society and the individual, in their striving to maintain stability, attempt to suppress [...] [Within this genre] all barriers are broken down and all secret spaces penetrated.'[12]

As we will see, Stevenson's *The Strange Case of Dr Jekyll and Mr Hyde* clearly exemplifies these deathless, disturbing and challenging traits.

---

[11] Hogle, p. 1.

[12] Glennis Byron, 'Introduction,' in *Dracula: New Casebooks* (Basingstoke: Macmillan, 1999), pp. 1-21 (p.2).

# Chapter One: The Story of the Door

Chapter One of *The Strange Case of Dr. Jekyll and Mr. Hyde* foregrounds many of the central ideas that filter through the novella in its entirety. Whilst the reader might expect the novella to focus immediately upon the character of Dr. Jekyll, as he is central to the title, Stevenson introduces us instead to the character of Utterson. It is significant that Stevenson does this; Utterson embodies some of the obstacles that Jekyll is revealed to be battling against during the novella.

As with the other Victorian gentleman in this novella, Utterson is having to manage his inner desires and pleasures against the backdrop of rigid and repressive social conventions that stifle individuality. Like Jekyll, rather than entirely wholesome, he is a mixture of good and bad, and this doubleness is central to Stevenson's vision: the individual is comprised of many, sometimes contradictory elements. As critic, Irving S. Saposnik points out:

> [Utterson] is introduced first not only because he is Jekyll's confidant [the only one remaining], but because by person and profession he represents the best and worst of Victoria's social beings. Pledged to a code harsh in its application, he has not allowed its pressures to mar his sense of human need. For himself he has chosen and he must make his life on that choice, yet he judges others with the understanding necessary

---

to human weakness.[13]

Indeed, the reader sees glimpses of what Saposnik labels as 'the best and worst of Victoria's social beings' from the first moment with meet Utterson:

> 'Mr. Utterson the lawyer was a man of rugged countenance, that was never lighted by a smile; cold, scanty and embarrassed in discourse; backward in sentiment; lean, long, dusty, dreary, and yet somehow lovable.'

Here, it is worth considering how Utterson is introduced to the reader; there is a clear emphasis on stiffness, ruggedness and formality. Mostly we see him from the outside; only a little light is shone onto his inner self. His first name remains hidden, hinting at the idea of secrecy and double lives that underpins the novella. The focus on Utterson's position and role - he is defined by being a lawyer - could also reflect the transactional nature of Late Victorian society, with status prioritised over individuality. His personal attributes are delayed to the end of the passage, signalling Stevenson's concern that emotions are suppressed or even sacrificed to the pretence of respectability.

In one way or another, all the Victorian gentleman in this novella and many novels of the period, are burdened by having to align with the strict social conventions of the day, with its values of moral earnestness, respectability, sobriety, industriousness, whilst finding ways to satisfy other needs. Repeatedly their appetites are driven underground, into private secret places, about which the morally upright figures feel

---

[13] Irving S. Saposnik, 'The Anatomy of Dr. Jekyll and Mr. Hyde,' *Studies in English Literature, 1500-1900*, Autumn, 1971. Volume 11. No. 4. Autumn 1971, pp. 715-731 (p. 719).

shame and guilt and are desperate to hide. No wonder then that Jekyll wishes to take to split the 'good and ill which divide and compound man's dual nature' liberating the public, good side of his character from his baser and disreputable desires.

The narrator establishes Utterson as possessing a hardened shell, 'a rugged countenance' with which to face the world. This shell is 'never lighted by a smile', presenting him as devoid of emotion and his demeanour as rather sombre. The adverb 'never' emphasises the permanence of this seriousness. Perhaps Utterson's sober demeanour shields him from the desires that enticed middle-class Victorian men. Utterson will play the role of detective in this 'case', a role we shall he is ill-suited for, though his leanness and serious appearance might signal the doggedness needed by any good detective.

Stevenson deliberately ends the list with a focus on 'lovable' to tap into a further concern that haunted the novelist as well as Victorian men as a whole: duality. Duality is the idea that beneath a surface unity lies a very different, divergent self. Perhaps Utterson is so 'austere with himself' because he fears what degrading desires might seep through his outer. In addition, his self-disciplined, regimented existence is further highlighted, when the narrator reveals that Utterson 'had not crossed the doors of [the theatre] for twenty years'. As theatres are epicentres of entertainment, which allow actors to adopt personas, whilst disguising their true nature, this avoidance seems significant and reflects Stevenson's idea that the authentic self of an individual lies beneath the surface of a socially constructed one. Like an actor on stage, Utterson alongside all the other Victorian gentlemen in the novella, are playing the part of respectable members of society, yet this is simply suppressing the uncivilised traits they keep under lock and key. Indeed, this tension is illuminated further in Chapter Two, as Utterson is completely repulsed about 'the many ill things he had done' confirming that he has his own dark secrets and shameful appetites he has repressed for the sake of preserving his social standing and reputation. The premodifiers 'many' and 'ill' demonstrate that these are not isolated incidents. As 'ill' is associated with sickness, it conveys his recognition that he has deviated from the rigid social conventions that he is expected to

follow. 'Things' is also vague – suggesting Utterson cannot or will not bring them fully to mind – further reflecting the theme of secrecy that underpins the novella. Such elusiveness encourages the reader to question: *What exactly has Utterson done? What is he so afraid of?*

Ultimately, from the outset, Stevenson is highlighting how Victorian gentlemen were, in fact, often tortured souls, oppressed by the very conventions that they propounded in public and they believed were holding society together. Whilst trying to follow strict social expectations, Victorian gentleman craved an authentic identity, which Saposnik notes led them to feeling 'haunted constantly by an inescapable sense of division'.[14] It is this 'inescapable sense of division' that Stevenson identifies as the source of self-destruction in the Victorian male psyche. It is no surprise then that Jekyll must take it upon himself to bring his 'unhappy [life] [...] to an end'.

Alongside Stevenson's introduction to the rational Utterson, the reader also meets the character of his friend, Enfield. Via Enfield the reader is

---

[14] Saposnik, p. 716.

first introduced to Hyde. According to one critic, Stevenson's sequence of 'individual narratives [helps to] provide [...] an increasing catalogue of attitudes towards Hyde's repulsiveness'.[15] In other words, Hyde's character is revealed through the lens of Enfield's perceptions, colouring our expectations before we can judge him for ourselves. In addition, the fact that Hyde does not have his own discrete chapter in the narrative in the same way as Jekyll does, further positions him as the outsider, and as secondary and dependent. As will be explored later, Hyde may indeed represent marginalised others within Victorian society, such as the working classes, with their lack of status reflected in the denial of his own chapter.

Enfield's character also offers another depiction of the Victorian gentleman. Mirroring Utterson, he seems to have his own inner demons and secret, hidden agendas. For instance, Enfield's revelations about his encounter with Hyde are ambiguous, to say the least. He notes that he was 'coming home from some place at the end of the world'. The adjective 'some' is suspiciously, elusively vague and unclear, indicating that the two characters may very well be acquainted. But Enfield is unwilling to go as far as to reveal exactly where he was or what he was doing there. This, in turn, suggests that he is guarding himself and his reputation in a similar way to Utterson. The phrase 'end of the world' also creates an apocalyptic image, and may represent Enfield as trawling the very depths of sin and desire, which was something that Stevenson himself acknowledged he was enticed by.[16] Moreover, Enfield notes that it was 'three o'clock of a

---

[15] Saposnik, p. 722.

[16] Christopher Frayling in *Nightmare: The Birth of Horror*, discusses that Stevenson's oppressive upbringing led him to feeling propelled to the darkness of the Old Town of Edinburgh, as it offered an outlet for releasing desires. It was the antithesis of the rigid existence offered by the New Town of Edinburgh.

black winter morning', thereby encouraging the reader to question Enfield's motivations for being around so late and in such blackness. *Why is he alone? Where had he been? What is he up to?* As with Utterson, there are more enigmas surrounding him than absolute certainties, which relates to the novella's central idea that nothing is as it first seems in this story and appearances may well be deceptive.

As will be explored later in this book, one potential reading that could explain the secrecy that underpins male characters is that they embody 'late Victorian anxieties about homosexuality', as 'Victorian sexology identified the homosexual as a perverse aberration and a degenerate'.[17] The 1885 Labouchère Amendment also increased these anxieties about homosexuality, as it meant 'sexual acts between men [were] illegal and punishable by imprisonment'.[18] If we take this queer reading, it is surely no coincidence that the male figures have secrets that they are unwilling to share, even with their closest friends, as revelation of their true sexuality would not only be scandalous, it would destroy their reputation. As Enfield succinctly points out in response to Hyde's actions: a 'gentleman [...] wishes to avoid a scene'.

Further evidence to support this queer reading includes the epithet used frequently to tag Hyde's character and actions, 'unspeakable'. One influential critic, Elaine Showalter, has opined that this is a code word for homosexual in Victorian culture. Later in the novel, we also consider the feminised description of another gentleman caught walking late in the small hours, alone in the Victorian streets and

---

[17] Kelly Hurley, 'British Gothic Fiction, 1885-1930,' in *The Cambridge Companion to Gothic Literature,* ed. by Jerrold E. Hogle, (Cambridge: Cambridge University Press, 2006), pp. 189-207 (p. 199).

[18] Hurley, p. 199.

fatefully accosting Hyde, Sir Danvers Carew.

Considering this, it is noteworthy that Hyde induces repulsion, as Enfield generates 'a loathing to [Hyde] a first sight', but that he is unable to articulate what exactly repels him. The best that Enfield can seem to do is state that Hyde has 'something wrong with his appearance; something displeasing; something downright detestable' and goes as far as to label him as 'deformed somewhere'. Perhaps, Enfield repeats 'something' because he fears stating explicitly what he sees in Hyde for the fear that it will unleash the desires that he himself is battling to suppress. Moreover, Enfield's inability to specifically define Hyde could also reflect the idea that Victorian society did not have a socially acceptable language to articulate and comprehend the subject of homosexuality. In this sense, Stevenson may be suggesting that Victorian society has its own evolutionary path to take.

A queer reading is not, however, the only interpretation of Hyde's character. His appearance generates abhorrence in all the characters who happen upon him. As a medical man, we would expect the Doctor to react in a calm and measured manner. However, instead he 'turned sick and white with the desire to kill him'. Hyde also drives the other characters around him into a sort of murderous frenzy - the women, for instance, become 'as wild as harpies'.

We could interpret this animalistic reaction of the crowd to Hyde as a kind of infection – contact with him leading to their wildness. Another way to look at, however, is in terms of Stevenson's presentation of degeneration. Victorian pseudo-science posited that atavistic types, such as criminals, could be identified through specific physical deformities, such as their facial features and the shape and size of their skulls. But the characters who encounter Hyde are not able to identify such specific features in him.

Perhaps, Stevenson seems to be implying, degeneracy is not as easily identifiable as the theorists suggest. How much more disturbing would it be if dangerous degenerates could mingle invisibly among innocent crowds? Moreover, what if degeneracy was not confined to particular types of people? Doesn't the crowd's instinctual, violent, animalistic response to Hyde suggests degeneracy might be found more widely in society than Utterson or his like can acknowledge?

Stevenson retains a sense of mystery about Hyde by not providing any physical description. However, we do learn that he moves through the city streets carelessly and destructively as a 'damned juggernaut' and that, consequently, he tramples a child into the ground. He also shows no remorse for this act of casual violence. As we will learn as the novella unfolds, Hyde embodies a range of Victorian fears, anxieties and desires. But the main thing we discover in this first encounter with him is how his presence appals and disgusts anyone unlucky enough to come across him. Appals them so much they want to tear him apart.

# Chapter Two: Search for Mr. Hyde

As the first chapter ends having established that the life of a Victorian gentleman is one of repression, Chapter Two takes us into the private sphere of Utterson to develop this idea further. The chapter begins with Utterson returning back to 'his bachelor house' in 'sombre spirits'. Here, the adjective 'sombre' reflects the similar feelings that he displayed in Chapter One. Stevenson indicates he is burdened by the constraints that Victorian society places upon him. The narrator states that:

> It was [Utterson's] custom of a Sunday, when the meal was over, to sit close by the fire, a volume of some dry divinity on his reading-desk, until the clock of the neighbouring church rang out the hour of twelve, when he would go soberly and gratefully to bed.

Utterson's existence is dictated by rigid customs, and Stevenson may be emphasising that it is the inability to break free from these dry, respectable routines that caused Victorian gentlemen to crave alternatives. The reference to 'the fire' may also represent the idea that this is the only warmth that he has in his rather cold life, as he does not experience warmth through the bonds he has with others, due to remaining detached. Perhaps, Stevenson is also hinting at another key concern; that the luxuries wealth and status bring do not necessarily deliver happiness and genuine comfort. Habitually Utterson is alone, isolated and is unhappy, perhaps, because of this.

Alongside the development of Utterson's character, the reader is also introduced to the antithesis of Jekyll: Dr. Lanyon. As with Utterson, his

---

character is defined by division. Lanyon may have an elegant exterior and it is noted that he appears a 'hearty, healthy, dapper, red-faced gentleman' yet has 'a shock of hair prematurely white'. As we will see later in the novella, this 'healthy' exterior will not last long, establishing how adversely Hyde threatens the stability of Victorian life. The phrase 'prematurely white' is important. It signals that the aging process has been accelerated for Lanyon. Stevenson may be indicating then that science has been the cause of this aging process; it is the first hint made to the reader that science is a potential danger to an individual if they become utterly absorbed by it. The adjective 'boisterous' used to describe Lanyon's manner signals his dual nature; the facade of respectability is contrasted with his potential for wildness and disorder. Indeed, this becomes more apparent as the chapter develops, as Lanyon displays a 'little spirit of tempter', illustrating that even he, who is regarded with the epithet 'great', has the capacity to be pettily unpleasant. Ultimately, as in Chapter One, Stevenson consistently presents characters composed of many layers, characters who are not at all as they first seem.

Through the introduction of Lanyon's character, the reader is also introduced to the conflict that has eroded his friendship with Jekyll. From the outset, Lanyon is quick to declare that he '[sees] little of [Jekyll] now', suggesting that he has deliberately distanced himself from Jekyll. Perhaps, Lanyon has also distanced himself, because he foresees the potential dangers ofJekyll's experiments. In particular, Lanyon may be detaching himself from Jekyll because he does not want to be tempted or have to confront what the experiments might reveal: i.e. the essentially dual nature of humanity. Indeed, this becomes apparent, when Lanyon states:

[Jekyll] began to go wrong, wrong in mind; and though, of

course, I continue to take an interest in him for old sake's sake as they say, I see and I have seen devilish little of the man. Such unscientific balderdash.

This passage demonstrates that disputes about the boundaries of science are the root cause of the fracturing of their friendship. Stevenson is suggesting that science, when ungoverned by ethical restraints, can not only be toxic to the individual, but can also have wider destructive consequences. The third person pronoun 'he', alongside the noun phrase 'the man' that Lanyon uses to label Jekyll also reflects a sense of detachment; it is almost like he cannot refer to Jekyll by name. The repetition of 'wrong', employed to describe

**Dangerous chemicals**

Jekyll's 'mind', also suggest that his obsession with pushing the boundaries of knowledge has turned him into a mad scientist, like Victor Frankenstein, as he now talks nothing but 'such unscientific balderdash'. This minor sentence highlights Lanyon's deep condemnation of the dangerous path that Jekyll has followed, as he is diverging from what Lanyon believes science should be. Whilst Stevenson is clearly tapping into anxiety about the potential of the chemical sciences here, Lanyon's reaction also reflects his own fears about what Jekyll's experiments might reveal about human nature, including his own nature.

In this sense, Lanyon's detachment from Jekyll is a small price to pay as it prevents him from having to confront what exists within himself. Perhaps he recognises that if Jekyll is successful with his pursuit of the 'transcendental', then it will lead to his own undoing.

Moreover, this chapter offers a further encounter with the uncivilised Hyde. But, unlike Chapter One, now it is the rational Utterson that interacts with him. Hyde is described as taking 'a hissing intake of [...]

breath', immediately evoking a snake, suggesting he might be venomous. Hyde may indeed be venomous to the Victorian gentleman, as well as the wider society, as he is destabilising the conventions that hold society together. He also 'snarled' like an aggressive predatory animal. Hyde responds to Utterson bluntly with 'What do you want?' implying he sees himself above and outside the social norms and etiquette that would be deemed necessary for a Victorian gentleman. Utterson is desperate to 'see [Hyde's] face' and this positions Hyde as having the capacity to attract as well as repulse. Whilst Utterson clearly wishes to identify Hyde, underlining Utterson's role as a detective figure in the novella – he tells us he is going to play 'Mr. Seek', his desire to look at Hyde's face could also suggest Hyde is a tempting force, as he roams freely without having to subdue desires.

This freedom is unlike the rest of the characters in this novella, as they rely on secrecy and suppression of emotion as a survival strategy. Hyde's instant 'flush of anger' establishes that he is violent and far from civilised; 'flush' might also represent the idea that it does not take much for his aggressive streak to come to the fore, indicating further that he is dangerously out-of-control and unpredictable. Though in some ways Hyde appears to be subhuman – Utterson thinks there is something of the cave-dweller about him, something 'troglodytic', he also moves with 'extraordinary quickness', suggesting he has superhuman powers.

This chapter is also crucial in that it establishes another possible reading of Hyde's character. Specifically Hyde may be an embodiment of anxieties about evolution that haunted late Victorian society. Nicholas Ruddick notes that the 'fin de siècle saw heightened cultural anxiety stemming from certain consequences of the Darwinian

---

revolution'.[19] Notably, it prompted the possibility that 'civilised human beings might revert atavistically to ancestral forms under the unprecedented stresses of modern life'.[20] Indeed, this is evinced in this chapter, as, in addition to being 'troglodytic' Hyde has a 'pale and dwarfish exterior'. While 'pale' suggests something sick or ghostly, 'dwarfish' indicates that the process of evolution has reversed and Hyde is an evolutionary throwback, a degenerate. What isn't yet clear is what sort of a degenerate Hyde is or what has caused him to degenerate. Deviance in Late Victorian society was often labelled as degenerate and we have already suggested that Hyde could represent homosexuality, as this was commonly demonized in the culture of the time. But Hyde's diminutive stature suggests that he could read as the embodiment of another fear, fear of the criminal classes. Consistently in Victorian medical and legal literature, criminals are labelled as degenerates, with their criminality claimed to be revealed by their warped and stunted appearance, their physiognomy.

Nicholas Ruddick looks to the Victorian poet, Alfred Lord Tennyson, to understand Hyde's presentation, stating that the poet believed 'moral progress [could be achieved by] allowing the inner ape [animal lust] and tiger [violence] to die', but Hyde exemplifies the 'modern man [whereby] the ape and tiger have been unleashed'.[21] It is no surprise then that Hyde triggers the same revulsion in Utterson as those that encountered him in Chapter One. Utterson is overwhelmed with 'unknown disgust, loathing and fear'. The syndetic list ends with 'fear',

---

[19] Nicholas Ruddick, 'The fantastic fiction of the fin de siècle,' in *The Cambridge Companion to The Fin de Siecle*, eds. by Gail Marshall, (Cambridge: Cambridge University Press, 2007), pp. 189-206 (p. 190).

[20] Ruddick, p. 191.

[21] Ruddick, p. 192.

signalling that Hyde may arouse questions about Utterson's own identity that he has avoided until now. In addition, 'unknown' is like 'something' when Utterson attempted to define Hyde earlier, suggesting that society does not yet possess the language or understanding to articulate the fears and desires Hyde embodies.

Disturbed in his dreams by a 'figure with no face' that haunts the 'wider labyrinths of the lamplighted city', Utterson takes up the detective role of 'Mr. Seek' in this chapter. Already, however, he seems as likely to be a 'Mr. Cover-Up'. Though he wrestles with the puzzle of the will and accosts Hyde in person, he is preoccupied with his friend's reputation. Moreover, Utterson too has buried secrets and 'was humbled to the dust by the many ill things he had done'. Like Jekyll, Utterson has a vested interest in not bringing some of these secret, ill things to the public's attention.

# Chapter Three: Dr. Jekyll was at Ease

Whilst the first two chapters focused on the unsettling nature of Hyde, Chapter Three focuses on Jekyll's character. An interesting parallel can be drawn here in that Hyde is introduced through the voice of Enfield and Utterson, which mirrors the way Jekyll is introduced. As with Hyde, this initial introduction creates an impression of the nature of his character before the reader can make their own judgement for themselves.

As expected of a Victorian gentleman with high social standing, Henry Jekyll provides 'one of his pleasant dinners' and is surrounded with 'all intelligent reputable men [who are] all judges of good wine'. There is a clear emphasis on luxury, comfort and consumption here. The noun phrase 'all intelligent reputable men' is significant, as it demonstrates that Jekyll's associates are all drawn from the upper echelons of society and should thus exemplify the conventions and etiquette of polite Victorian society. However, if someone as 'austere' as Utterson withholds the truth about himself and has secrets of his own that he detests, we are prepped to eye this circle of seemingly respectable men with the same suspicion. Continually, Stevenson insinuates that the appearance of Victorian gentleman as morally upright and 'reputable' is only a social performance of identity, a projection, a façade. The focus on them as 'intelligent' is also important, as we see later in the novella through the revelation that Jekyll and Hyde are indeed the same person that intelligence does not necessarily equate with virtue nor with evolutionary development.

Shockingly for its contemporary readers, the novella opines that even cultured, respectable Victorian gentlemen can, in fact, regress down the evolutionary chain – in Victorian culture this was known as degeneration - as reflected through Hyde's primitive, 'troglodytic', 'ape-like' and 'dwarfish' exterior.

The opening of the chapter also illuminates the sharp gender divide that was central to Victorian society. So far the novella has featured no female characters. The world of Utterson, Lanyon and Jekyll is a markedly homosocial one, almost entirely male only. The absence of female characters could reflect the Victorian notion of the Separate Spheres, whereby men played an active role, whilst women were  expected to accept a domesticated one. However, during the *sin-de-siècle* period, women started to reject their domestic restraints and to agitate for more rights and a powerful new figure, the New Woman, arrived on the scene. Inevitable questions about identity arose and the previously strict binary divisions of the Separate Spheres began to loosen. Perhaps, the way that Stevenson's male characters are united together in exclusively male company reflects wider attempts in the culture to prevent women from invading male private territory. The novella has already established a focus on male-to-male interactions, and the way that this continues within the private sphere in this chapter may also reflect the possibility of homosexuality.

This chapter also introduces the reader to the physical description of Jekyll, as well as his thoughts and feelings towards Lanyon and Hyde. According to one critic, it is important to look underneath the outer layer of appearance, as Stevenson does not 'focus [solely] on the physical appearance of the characters, but rather [exposes] their personalities and mental conditions'.[22]

Indeed, this is evident in the initial portrayal of Jekyll, as the narrator introduces him as:

> 'a large, well-made, smooth-faced man, with something a stylish cast perhaps, but every mark of capacity and kindness – you could see by his looks that he cherished for Mr. Utterson a sincere and warm affection.'

Whilst 'large' could represent his dominance and perhaps his influence upon those around him, 'well-made' positions him as the potential embodiment of the evolved Victorian gentleman. As with Utterson and Lanyon earlier, there is a notable contrast evident in Jekyll's introduction, which hints as his dual nature. 'Smooth-faced' makes him seem clear of imperfections, but it also suggests an element of performance and concealment – the hiding of one's true identity under a layer of affability. Like Hyde's initial introduction, 'something' is attached to Jekyll, which establishes the idea that even though he is recognisable as Jekyll, there are layers to his character that remain mysterious and cannot be totally defined. The adjective 'stylish' that pre-modifies 'cast' demonstrates he has the potential to be sinister. His tendency to be 'stylish' is clearly part of his nature, and it indicates to the reader that he makes a conscious effort to project himself in certain ways. Meanwhile, with its connection to acting, 'cast' also hints at potential duplicity.

---

[22] URSZULA CZYŻEWSKA and GRZEGORZ GŁĄB, 'Robert Louis Stevenson Philosophically: Dualism and Existentialism within the Gothic Conventions,' *Roczniki Filozoficzne / Annales de Philosophie / Annals of Philosophy*, 2014, Vol. 62, No. 3 (2014), pp. 19-33 (p. 21).

Whereas in Chapter Two we learned about Lanyon's grounds for concern over Jekyll's 'unscientific balderdash', Chapter Three offers a contrasting position. Here Jekyll outlines why he is at odds with Lanyon. He labels Lanyon a 'hide-bound pedant' and claims he has 'never [been] more disappointed in any man than Lanyon'. Stevenson employs Lanyon as a foil for Jekyll, and they represent alternative approaches to science. As a critic states, Jekyll 'embodies the 19th century ambitions and illusions' that 'resulted in the cult of science'.[23] Considering this, it is no surprise then that Jekyll labels Lanyon as a 'hide-bound pedant' and repeatedly does so. Unlike Jekyll, Lanyon will not abuse his position as a scientist by pushing his experiments into dangerous, unethical territory, which frustrates the more ambitious, or desperate, Jekyll. Stevenson is also tapping into a wider dichotomy at the heart of late nineteenth century British culture between those refusing to adapt and embrace new ideas and those wishing to break boundaries for the sake of knowledge. Essentially, Lanyon represents the cautious scientist, whilst Jekyll embodies the scientist who, like Dr. Faustus and Victor Frankenstein, refuses to limit his search for knowledge.

Through this past clash between Jekyll and Lanyon, Stevenson delivers a clear warning about the dangers of transgression and tapping into the unknown forces of nature. For the moment, Lanyon's detachment from Jekyll has shielded him, yet Jekyll becomes increasingly absorbed by the undiscovered areas of science, an obsession that leads to the undoing of both himself and those around him. Stevenson's portrayal of Jekyll is like that of Victor in Mary Shelley's *Frankenstein* [1818] in that they both become hubristic, and they both experience the same consequence: destruction of others and, finally, self-destruction.

---

[23] Urszula Czyżewska and Grzegorz Głąb, p. 22-24.

Despite the chapter being titled 'Dr. Jekyll was quite at ease,' by the end, it becomes apparent that this is a pivotal moment for Jekyll and that his existence will never be the same again. Ironically, the hubristic Jekyll reassures Utterson that he 'can be rid of Hyde' at any moment. Of course the very opposite occurs as the novella unfolds. Indeed, Jekyll acknowledges this in his confession during Chapter Ten, as he was 'slowly losing hold of [his] original and better self, and [was] becoming slowly incorporated with my second and worse'. Jekyll's revelation at the end of the chapter that he 'only [asks] for justice […] when [he] is no longer here' foreshadows his own demise and makes it seem inevitable that his pursuit of science will lead to this. It is as though Jekyll is acutely aware of the calculated risks that he is taking by pursuing the unknown. Altogether then, it is significant that the chapter begins with a focus on comfort, yet ends on a note of death. This prepares the reader for the turbulent battle that Jekyll will have with the darker half of his psyche, interestingly described here as a 'young man'.

# Chapter Four: The Carew Murder Case

This chapter exemplifies how the Gothic genre shapeshifts over time, mutating in response to changing contexts. Unlike early Gothic fiction, such as Horace Walpole's *The Castle of Otranto* [1764], Stevenson's novella does not use a medieval setting in a faraway land. Rather it brings the Gothic into the very heart of Victorian society. In this sense,

Stevenson is aligning with other writers of the time. Bram Stoker, in *Dracula* [1898] introduces the possibility of the dangerous outsider in the form of a vampire invading Victorian society, whilst Oscar Wilde's *The Picture of Dorian Gray* [1890] explores the same concept of duality as Stevenson does. The Gothic violence of this chapter happens in a real, actual place, a 'dismal quarter of Soho', uncomfortably close, for contemporary readers, to home and London, the centre of empire and bastion of civilization appears to the unimaginative Utterson to have become 'some city in a nightmare'

It is significant that there has been a passing of time, as in this chapter, the narrator notes that it was 'nearly a year later'. The creates another enigma. We are left to question what has happened in between. The passing of time is key in terms of portraying the malevolent growth of Hyde. Now '[trampling] calmly' is not enough to satisfy his appetite for violence; now he commits a ferocious and brutal murder.

The late nineteenth century, the period known as the *fin de siècle*, was an era riddled with anxiety and uncertainty, especially as the conventions that held society together were being questioned and challenged. The prospect of a murder being committed by a seemingly upright and respectable gentleman would inspire insecurity and fear. On top of that the victim was not a low-life criminal, but a gentleman and knight of the realm. The way that London is personified as being 'startled by a crime of singular ferocity' demonstrates perhaps the myopia of Victorian thinking; such monstrous acts being committed by and on a gentleman was unthinkable. Ultimately, in the context of the novella, the violence undermines the foundations of Victorian life, like an earthquake. As the action unfolds, the characters have to face the aftershocks of the discovery that evil lurks not just within their own society, but within their own elevated class. As will be considered later in the book, one potential reading of Hyde is that he is an embodiment of fears about the working class. His violent outbreak could perhaps symbolise the possibility of an underclass taking revenge upon the upper classes that have marginalised and exploited them.

A stark contrast between Carew and Hyde is also revealed in this chapter. Carew is depicted as 'an aged and beautiful gentleman' with 'very pretty manners of politeness'. Both adjectives are more commonly ascribed to female characters, hinting, perhaps, at something feminine in Carew's character. His delicate attributes are the exact opposite to those that Hyde displays: 'And then all of a sudden be broke out in a great flame of anger, stamping with his foot, brandishing his cane, and carrying on […] like a madman'.

Obviously, the phrase 'all of a sudden' portrays the unpredictable nature of Hyde, and it conveys the idea that the uncivilised nature of man cannot be controlled or constrained once it has been unleashed. Likewise, the plosive 'broke' emphasises the surge and intensity of his rampage and the violence released. 'Stamping' is also reminiscent of how he treated the young girl in Chapter One, but stamping also implies leaving a mark, which could represent a role reversal - it is the uncivilized or underclass stamping their power on things. The image of a 'flame' is also noteworthy, as the destruction caused by fire travels far and wide, which signifies how Hyde's violence will have wider repercussions. Flames also eventually burn out or are extinguished, hinting that this outburst will die out. The simile 'like a madman' also illustrates that he is at odds with Victorian society, is out of control and lacks any sense of normal decency. The pattern of present participle verbs with 'stamping,' 'brandishing,' and 'trampling' also demonstrates Hyde's unwillingness to stop until he is no longer reminded of what he has, perhaps, grown to despise.

If we adopt this position, the attack upon Sir Danvers Carew forces the reader to question exactly why Hyde attacked him. What does Hyde detest in Carew? Perhaps, he does not wish to be reminded of what Sir Danvers Carew exemplifies: the etiquette and conventions that all Victorian gentleman were expected to follow. Perhaps he sees in his victim everything that he is not. Or perhaps the hostility springs from class conflict, the underclass taking its revenge on the aristocratic.

Throughout Hyde's attack, there is a pattern of gruesome and violent imagery that demonstrates how much Hyde has deteriorated. His capacity for evil has grown and is far more malicious than it was earlier. The way 'he broke out of all bounds' and delivers 'a storm of blows' emphasises how he cannot be contained any longer, cannot, in fact, contain himself, and would, perhaps, frighten a Victorian reader, inviting them to question whether they might have the same bestial traits buried somewhere within themselves. 'Storm' is effective, as it portrays Hyde as causing disorder and chaos. However, more reassuringly, a storm is only temporary and eventually fades. The fact that Hyde delivers multiple 'blows' to Carew demonstrates his unwillingness to stop until he obliterates any reminder of Victorian gentility.

Although the Jack the Ripper murders occurred after the publication of the novella, Stevenson's description of the killing of Sir Danvers Carew seems to anticipate the possibility of such brutal crimes taking place in contemporary London. In a strange, but telling twist, the author of the stage play of the novella, Richard Mansfield, was later accused of actually being Jack the Ripper, apparently in part due to the authentic transformation scenes within the play.[24] Contemporary coverage of the murders initially assumed that the killer was a monstrous degenerate bred in the London slums, a revealing example of Victorian social prejudices.

Whilst in previous chapters Hyde was simply hated, he is now branded as a 'murderer'. Simply inflicting pain, sadism, is not enough now to quench his savage thirsts. The description of Carew as being positioned in 'the middle of the lane' could perhaps symbolise the idea

that Hyde sees Carew as an obstacle. It also represents the idea that the repressed nature of man, once free, will not remain subdued and will overthrow what was once dominant. Leaving Carew 'incredibly mangled' has connotations of entanglement, and reflects the savage and gruesome attack, but could also reflect the way the nature of the Victorian gentleman has itself been mangled. This is emphasised further through the 'heavy cane,' which is part of the attire of the Victorian gentleman.

---

[24] https://www.bl.uk/collection-items/richard-mansfield-in-the-role-of-jekyll-and-hyde

The way this had 'broken in the middle under the stress of this insensate cruelty' is surely symbolic of the rejection of the conventions that repressed Jekyll in the first place. Alternatively, the way the cane has fractured into two halves could also symbolise the splintering of good and evil within society. Even more so, a cane acts as a support structure, and Hyde's destruction of it may signal that he longer needs to depend on the conventions that help define his other, better self, Dr. Jekyll.

The officer's reaction to the death of Carew is also loaded with duality. He says 'Good God Sir! Is it possible?' one moment and then he 'lighted up with professional ambition'. The verb 'lighted' suggests that he has been invigorated by this immoral act, whilst it also portraying him as an opportunist, as he will use the case to promote his career. Ultimately, this forces the reader to address the unsettling idea that the traits displayed by those around us, including those on whom we expect to trust, such as those involved with the law – lawyers and policemen - could in fact be false and that darker motives may reside beneath trustworthy exteriors.

Hyde remains a mysterious character in this chapter. His motives are mysterious - we do not learn why he attacked his victim. He is also elusive - when Utterson and the officer track him to his dwelling, they are unable to apprehend him. Indeed, Hyde seems to have no history, no family, and he has 'never been photographed'. The anonymous nature of Hyde adds to the enigma, but also to the fear inspired by his character. He's like a ghost, slipping through the nightmare city, leaving no trace other than the violence he inflicts on his victims. And because no-one is able to describe what he looks like and have no photographs or documents to identify him he could be any stranger you happen to pass, with a shudder, in the city streets.

# Chapter Five: Incident of the Letter

In this chapter, Utterson visits Jekyll and the reader is allowed into the mysterious inner space of Jekyll's laboratory, the scene of his transformations. The way that 'the laboratory or the dissecting-rooms' is detached across a yard which had 'once been a garden' suggests perhaps how science is overwriting all that went before it. Certainly the laboratory is separated from the house, the home space, as if what goes on there is not entirely respectable. Of course, a 'dissecting-room' is associated with experimentation, but also specifically with the taking of things apart, which may also reflect Jekyll's intentions to access his uncivilised self and remove that.

The description of the laboratory is also important in establishing the potential consequences of unregulated scientific experimentation. It's a 'dingy windowless structure', an isolated space with an uneasy, uncanny feel to it that makes the rational Utterson feel discomfort and distaste. The morally dark, dubious things that are taking place here and their mysterious qualities are indicated by references to the half-light – 'dingy', 'dimly', 'foggy' – words with which also reflect Utterson's uncertain perceptions. The 'windowless' nature of the environment hints at secrets and signals the idea that once an individual becomes obsessed by science, it can shut them in and shut the world out. The contrast of the laboratory in that it was once 'crowded with eager students' and is now 'gaunt and silent' creates the idea of decay and reflects the wider corruption at play in society. The personification of also gives the laboratory a ghost-like, liminal dimension.

---

Again, striking parallels can be made to Victor in Mary Shelley's *Frankenstein*, as both Victor and Jekyll undergo transformations; both did not expect the pursuit of science to be their undoing; hubristically in their pursuit of new discoveries both resisted all attempts at restraint; both are classic Gothic overreachers usurping the role of both women and of God. The phrase 'deadly sick' emphasises the repercussions of Jekyll's experiments, while 'cold hand' and 'a changed voice' also reflect his deterioration and loss of vigour. This weakened man is no longer the renowned Henry Jekyll. Indeed, the changed nature of Jekyll is exposed later in the chapter through his exchanges with Utterson. His once confident exterior has now collapsed into anxiety and concern. He is aware of the terrible repercussions that being Hyde has brought upon him, as he states that 'this hateful business has exposed', much though he did not want his hidden self to be revealed in the public sphere. 'Business' again hides the precise truth about what Jekyll has been conducting behind closed doors, whilst 'exposed' signals that Jekyll is now under the limelight and Hyde is both tarnishing his reputation and eating away at his sense of self. What is more, like Victor in *Frankenstein*, the consequences of an unfettered pursuit of forbidden knowledge are becoming abundantly clear, as he states that he has 'lost confidence in himself'. Moreover, his epiphany has taught him the tragic errors of his ways. Usurping God comes with at a terrible price: a deep existential dread that shakes the core of his being almost to pieces.

Clearly, Jekyll has become a victim of his infatuation with science and in the process, he has nearly lost himself. As he declares 'I have had a lesson – O God, Utterson, what a lesson I have had!' He has discovered something, learnt something, but this has traumatised Jekyll. He has peered beneath the refined exterior of the Victorian gentleman and looked into the eyes of the beast within. More than that, he has tasted

 what it is like to be that beast, part him even revelling in the wild liberation. But another part of him, his better half, is morally appalled. And frightened too. Now that Hyde has been released, Jekyll begins to fear that it will not be so easy to put him back in his cage.

Jekyll's reversal of fortune demonstrates that science does not always bring about good and mirrors similar concerns that other writers from the same period, such as H.G. Wells, expressed. Writers like Wells were deeply worried about complacent Victorian assumptions that held men had a God-like position in society that could not be challenged.

Jekyll's view of Hyde is very different now from how he felt in Chapter Three. In this chapter, Jekyll totally rejects and repudiates his other self, forcefully declaring 'I swear to God I will never set eyes on him again [...] I am done with him in this world. It is all at an end'. The modal verb 'will' and the adverb 'never' work together to illustrate the finality of his decision. However, as we soon discover, this firm resolution is short-lived. Despite his apparently good intentions, base desires and appetites are not so easy to shrug off once they have been indulged. Jekyll is like a drug addict; one moment renouncing the Hyde drug and going clean, the next minute caving into its temptations and relapsing. His refusal to 'set eyes' on Hyde may convey a sense of bitter disgust and repulsion, and reflect the idea that he does not want to be reminded about what lives within himself, but it is also a refusal to properly acknowledge his true self, with its demeaning imperfections. Rather than liberating Jekyll's good half into saintly serenity, becoming Hyde has made him hate himself even more. The bluntness of the simple sentence, 'It was all at an end' marks the end of their mutual co-existence, perhaps, but has wider, more ominous resonances. Again, a striking parallel can be drawn between Victor Frankenstein and Jekyll here, as they both abandon their own creations and suffer the murderous consequences.

Whatever Jekyll's attempts to wrestle back control of himself and bury his demon, Hyde is becoming more powerful and malignant. Jekyll states that Hyde is becoming more independent – he 'does not want my help', and as will be explored later in the book, one potential reading of the Jekyll and Hyde relationship could be as a father-son one. Hence perhaps the earlier to reference to Hyde as being like young man. After all, Stevenson himself was frustrated with the oppressive upbringing shaped by his father. Considering this, Hyde's unwillingness to have Jekyll's 'help' may represent the way that a child gradually moves from dependency to embracing liberation and independence.

Once again, Utterson's behaviour raises some serious ethical issues, undermining his role as an investigator. Jekyll tells him, for instance, about Hyde disappearing from London. Shouldn't an upstanding member of the public and, moreover, a lawyer report this to the police? Shouldn't Jekyll at least be questioned about the recent brutal murder? At the end of this chapter, the relationship between Utterson and his clerk, Mr. Guest, is revealed and it is Guest, not Utterson, who spots the cluse of the similarity between Jekyll and Hyde's handwriting. Despite the evidence being right in front of the supposedly intelligent Utterson, he does make the connection that Jekyll and Hyde exist in the same body. While for a modern reader, this alone might make Utterson seem a rather inadequate detective figure, to be fair to him, it would have taken a huge leap of the imagination to put this particular two and two together.

For the original readers, of course, the fact that Jekyll is Hyde would not have been at all obvious until the very end of the novella. Making the hero figure also the villain was a brilliant and startling innovation within the Gothic by Stevenson. More than that, this move, probably influenced by the work of the psychologist Sigmund Freud, turned Hyde into an even more disturbing figure for Victorian readers. Not only can Hyde be seen to be an embodiment of the homosexual, the fear of reverse evolution, a criminal, the working class and the anonymous, dangerous, metropolitan stranger, far more troublingly, he is also the stranger within - the self as monstrous other, the terrifying, uncanny double.

# Chapter Six: Incident of Dr. Lanyon

From the outset of this chapter, the true horror of Hyde's character is made explicit. He is defined by his 'cruelty', by being 'so callous', he is 'violent' and 'vile'. Every layer of his being is, it seems, unequivocally evil. However, while society grows increasingly resentful over the death of Sir Danvers Carew, Hyde seems to have 'never existed'. This causes the reader to question where has Hyde gone? What has Jekyll done to subdue Hyde? Noticeably too, our detective figure, Utterson, happy that Hyde seems to have disappeared, loses his appetite to solve the 'case'.

It is no coincidence that as Hyde seems to go underground, Jekyll's former self has been restored. The noun phrase 'a new life' demonstrates that he has almost symbolically been reborn and has been given a new chance to begin again, especially as the adjective 'new' is associated with freshness. On the other hand, 'new' suggests that the burdens that haunted Jekyll's past may have been temporarily lifted. Like Victor in Shelley's *Frankenstein*, once Jekyll has moved away from science, he emerges from 'his seclusion', whilst 'renew[ing] relations with his friends', he becomes 'once more their familiar guest and entertainer'. 'Entertainer' perhaps hints that this return to his old self and to his old conviviality might be something of a performance. An entertainer will perform to please the audience regardless of their own feelings at the time, which reflects Jekyll's situation. 'Open' and 'brightened' are used to describe Jekyll's facial expressions, contrasting markedly with the 'deadly sick' exterior that Utterson observed in Chapter Five.

---

Without a doubt, Stevenson is continuing to emphasise that an obsessive fascination with science has the potential to cripple an individual, especially when science is used as a tool to usurp the role of God.

Structurally, the chapter seems to demonstrate that Jekyll's rebirth will be short-lived. Only a few paragraphs after Jekyll's 'new' exterior had been noted, Poole states that his master has suddenly withdrawn again from society and secluded himself at home: Jekyll has 'confined' himself to the house and sees 'no one'. This illustrates his movement from freedom back into isolation once more; it also prepares the reader for the re-emergence of Hyde, as Jekyll's detaching of himself from those around him is signal of Hyde's refusal to remain repressed.

In this chapter, Stevenson also highlights how science can have wide scale consequences that go far beyond the individual. Utterson's visit to Lanyon demonstrates this. Lanyon is on death's door; the 'rosy man had grown pale, his flesh had fallen away; he was visibly balder and older'. The contrast between the adjective 'rosy' and 'pale' illustrates that he has started to lose blood, to lose vigour. It is almost as though his association with Jekyll, and thus Hyde, has activated his own internal degeneration - his flesh having 'fallen away' as if decomposing and withering. Also, the comparatives 'balder' and 'older' present Lanyon undergoing his own physical transformation as well as mental one, and it reflects Stevenson's idea that unregulated science can be toxic to the soul. However, Lanyon's sudden decrepitude invites the reader to ask: Why has Hyde had such a profoundly enervating effect upon him?

Throughout the chapter, Lanyon is repeatedly portrayed as insecure and beset by internal struggles. He has come to have a 'deep-seated terror of the mind' and he is quick to label himself as 'a doomed man'.

He confesses to Utterson that:

> 'I have had a shock [...] I shall never recover. It is a question of weeks. Well, life has been pleasant; I liked it; yes, sir, I used to like it. I sometimes think if we knew all, we should be more glad to get away.'

Certainly, Lanyon is no longer the 'hide-bound pedant' that Jekyll categorised him as earlier. Neither does Lanyon display the same 'boisterous and decided manner'. Perhaps, Hyde has illuminated the very attributes that Lanyon has repressed for so long that he can no longer deny their existence within him. Alternatively, if we apply a 'queer' reading of the text, maybe his 'deep-seated terror' and his feeling that he is on the brink of death may be due to the fear of having to confront his own sexuality. Or is it just that he has seen Jekyll transform into Hyde and this has shaken him so because such a transformation undermines every understanding he had of the nature of human identity? His acceptance that his death is 'a question of weeks' and that once 'we [know] all' about ourselves, reflects Stevenson's concerns about the consequences of repressing inner demons. Through Lanyon, as through Hyde, the novelist may be demonstrating how repression of our desires only makes them even more potent and destructive once released.

Lanyon's deterioration then is similar to Jekyll's. As David Punter argues, 'the real problem is not the existence of some more primitive and passionate internal self, but the force with which that self must be repressed in accordance with social conventions'.[25] Considering Punter's assessment, perhaps Lanyon cannot carry on abiding by

---

[25] David Punter, 'Gothic and Decadence' in *The Gothic*, (Oxford: Blackwell Publishing, 2004), pp. 39-43 (p. 41).

outdated social norms, whilst Hyde embodies the attractive potential that transgression offers to the Victorian gentleman. Alternatively, the experience has undermined Lanyon's fundamental understanding of the nature of the world and, specifically, the integrity of the individual. Yet, it could also reflect the idea that Lanyon has learnt the true state of society, and that beneath the façade of Victorian respectability lies a sickening core.

Whilst the clash between Jekyll and Lanyon resurfaces in this chapter, they clearly find solace with one thing: they are better detached from each other. As highlighted in this chapter, hearing Jekyll's name is enough to trigger Lanyon's 'trembling hand'. Lanyon also 'regard[s] [Jekyll] as dead' which highlights how severely their relationship deteriorated. Perhaps, keeping Jekyll away from him will make his last days more tolerable in that he will not have to remember what exists within himself or within others. Likewise, Jekyll also sees the relationship as 'incurable', as diseased and impossible to fix. Ultimately, this demonstrates how releasing secrets and utilising science to explore the unknown avenues of human nature can lead to irreparable divisions.

Finally, it is significant that as the chapter develops, the more alienated Jekyll becomes. Alongside this, the way that Lanyon dies within 'a fortnight' prepares us for Jekyll's own fate. It also seems that Jekyll may be aware of his own impending doom when he prepares Utterson:

> 'You must suffer me to go my own dark way. I have brought on myself a punishment and a danger that I cannot name. If I am the chief of sinners, I am the chief of sufferers also.'

Jekyll's acceptance that he must continue this plight may also illustrate he can suppress the Hyde part of his self and its savage appetites no longer. This is a dark path that he must follow through himself, regardless of the end consequences. Like Lanyon, Jekyll's tampering with science haunts him. And, just as the characters who come across Hyde struggle to describe and categorise him, so too Jekyll 'cannot name' what he has unleashed in himself. 'Cannot', of course, carries both the sense of 'not able to' and 'will not allow himself to' so there is ambiguity here about the extent to which Jekyll is able to understand what he has done.

Even more so, the unnameable nature of Hyde demonstrates how society, even with the scientific advances, has not evolved enough yet

and does not have the capacity to comprehend the nature of his specific darkness. The syntactical parallelism in the final sentence of this passage with, 'If I am the chief of sinners, I am the chief of suffers also' is noteworthy as it is loaded with contrast and duality. It reinforces

Stevenson's central idea that we are all a mixture of elements, rather than being one dimensional, good or bad. The way in which Jekyll also sees himself as both sinner and sufferer signals how he is torn between having to comply with societal expectations, whilst battling with his own desires. A 'chief' leads the way, which positions Jekyll as the embodiment of all that society has tried to repress.

# Chapter Seven: Incident at the Window

We seem to have come full circle. Utterson and Enfield are together again and Utterson is completing 'his usual walk'. Whilst this chapter begins on a note of repetitiveness and a return to familiar routines, it certainly does not end this way.

Unlike previous chapters, the well-respected, eminent Jekyll seems to be viewed differently now by those around him. The epithet 'poor' to describe 'Jekyll' hints that his experiments have not delivered the benefits he so desperately craved. Instead, 'poor' suggests he has become a pitiable shell of his former self. As one critic has pointed out, the novella is primarily about '19th century ambitions and illusions'[26] and this chapter is pivotal in demonstrating how Jekyll's ambitions have failed.

Increasingly he has become isolated, withdrawn and detached, remaining confined within the private sphere, like a 'disconsolate prisoner'. Through him, Stevenson indicates the consequences of adopting a God-like role as a creator, as well as warning against moving too quickly and freely with science. Science brings great unhappiness for Jekyll and also for those in his circle.

As David Punter in *The Gothic* argues, the novella 'engages with and

---

[26] URSZULA CZYŻEWSKA and GRZEGORZ GŁĄB, 'Robert Louis Stevenson Philosophically: Dualism and Existentialism within the Gothic Conventions,' *Roczniki Filozoficzne / Annales de Philosophie / Annals of Philosophy*, 2014, Vol. 62, No. 3 (2014), pp. 19-33 (p. 21).

aggravates cultural anxieties about the dangers associated with scientific progress, particularly if such progress is not directed by clear moral guidelines'.[27]

The simile 'like some disconsolate prisoner' is significant. It demonstrates that he is not just unhappy, but trapped. Whatever sordid pleasures he may have enjoyed as Hyde, he has ended up imprisoned by this other self. This may indicate that regardless of what one is willing to change within oneself, society plays a fundamental part in shaping our lives. Jekyll, therefore, is perhaps a victim of the conventions that held the Victorian gentleman in place. He cannot freely be his other self, because that self is demonised by society. As David Punter points out, Jekyll is the 'the product of a particular historical moment, when the strict policing of morality needed to uphold the sense of Victorian middle-class superiority inevitably resulted in the intensification of various psychic pressures'.[28]

Not even his experimental science has offered Jekyll a remedy, a way to out of the straight jacket of convention or relief from psychic

pressures. Perhaps such relief is impossible to achieve unless society and its conventions alter. This moment may also reflect wider social issues surrounding the treatment of madness and insanity, as the nineteenth century led a 'rapid expansion of an asylum system designed "mercifully to control" the insane', whilst there was a 'nagging fear that persons were being improperly

---

[27] David Punter, 'Robert Louis Stevenson *Dr Jekyll and Mr Hyde* (1886),' in *The Gothic*, (Oxford: Blackwell Publishing, 2004), pp. 226-229 (pp. 227-228).

[28] David Punter, p. 228.

confined in asylums.'[29] Perhaps then, Jekyll's imprisonment acts as a reminder of what one critic labels as 'lunacy panics'[30] of the nineteenth century. Controversially Stevenson seems to be suggesting that violent insanity can emerge from the distinguished, upper echelons of society.

Jekyll's confident and restored exterior, revealed in Chapter Six, has been short-lived. Once the uncivilised Hyde has been unleashed, the novella suggests, it is impossible to keep him contained. Jekyll confesses that he is 'very low', an image that hints at degeneration. Obviously, Jekyll's acknowledgement that he is 'low' suggests he is depressed and that his mental health has been compromised, but such lowness could also reflect wider social anxieties surrounding class reversal. If we take Jekyll as the embodiment of the wealthy upper-class men of the day, and Hyde as the repressed working class, Jekyll feeling 'low' suggests he has been brought down by this alter ego.

The description of Jekyll's home is important. The narrator notes that 'the middle one of the three windows was half-way open'. The fact that the middle window is 'half-way' open reflects Jekyll's half-way, liminal state. Like the setting of the scene, its 'premature twilight', Jekyll is stuck, caught midway between his past self and his darker side. Jekyll is also behind a window, notnot directly making contact with the outside world. A window cancan distort what is on the other side of it, which may also represent Jekyll's unstable, fluctuating identity.

In keeping with Gothic tradition, the final events of this chapter create

---

[29] Peter McCandless, 'Dangerous to Themselves and Others: The Victorian Debate over the Prevention of Wrongful Confinement,' *Journal of British Studies*, Autumn, 1983, Vol. 23, No. 1 (Autumn, 1983), pp. 84-10 (p. 84).

[30] Peter McCandless, p. 84.

fear and dread. Utterson and Enfield witness an 'expression of such abject terror and despair' on Jekyll's face that

it 'froze' their 'very blood'. 'Froze' reflects the paralysis that whatever horror they've witnessed has induced, while the idea of their 'very blood' freezing suggests the sight may even be life threatening. Perhaps, briefly spying some sort of uncanny transformation in Jekyll has disturbed them to the core of their beings, as it did Lanyon. A key characteristic of the Gothic is its design to unnerve and unsettle in this way.

Why does Utterson end the chapter exclaiming 'God forgive us!' twice? During the late nineteenth century religious beliefs were being challenged, not least through the idea of evolution. This period has been labelled as the 'Age of Doubt', as a time where society suffered a profound 'Crisis of Faith'. As a lawyer, Utterson is a man of reason. Whatever he sees in this chapter shakes him that he turns to God. 'Us' is the interesting word. 'God forgive him' would have expressed what we might have expected. 'Us', however, implicates Utterson somehow in the horror. Why does Utterson need forgiveness? What dark secrets has Utterson been keeping under his hat?

# Chapter Eight: The Last Night

Immediately, the title of the chapter foregrounds the events that it will unfold. The adjective 'last' signals finality, perhaps preparing the reader for the inevitable demise of Jekyll, while 'night' is associated with darkness and reinforces the Gothic trope of gloom and the unknown. The chapter begins with Poole – Jekyll's loyal servant – who reveals that his master is 'shut up again in the cabinet', illustrating that Jekyll is having to confine himself once more. As noted in previous chapters, it is ironic that Jekyll has been rendered a prisoner through tampering with the very thing that he thought would bring about his release. From this, Stevenson is clearly maintaining one consistent message that runs throughout the novella: irresponsible dabbling in science has the direst of consequences.

Poole is in a state of panic, demonstrating genuine concern for his master. He is also fearful of his own safety. Poole goes as far as to wish the worst possible scenario upon himself, as he 'wish[es] [he] may die' and his frank acknowledgement that he is 'afraid' signals a stark difference between the lower and upper classes. Poole's admission demonstrates that he is in tune with his feelings and is not afraid to articulate them, which is something that the Victorian gentlemen in the novella struggle to do. Hyde causes the same trauma in Poole, as he inflicts on everyone else, as Poole is described as having a 'manner [...] altered for the worst', highlighting the unsettling nature of Hyde.

Like Guest, Poole can see what is taking place around him. He suspects 'foul play'. Stevenson is continuing to highlight here how the pretensions of Victorian society seem to shroud Victorian gentlemen from seeing what is in front of them. In contrast to Poole, Utterson continues to ignore the truth. He even seems perplexed: 'What foul play? What does the man mean?' Indeed, this becomes even more evident when Poole states that 'Mr. Utterson, you are a hard man to satisfy' when Utterson believes Poole's concerns are nothing more than a 'very strange' and 'wild' 'tale'. Utterson is complacent here, and once again he seems an inadequately motivated detective. It seems unlikely that, left to his own devices, that he would ever have cracked the 'strange case'.

We are also introduced to the important symbol of 'the red baize' in this chapter. This material covers 'the cabinet door' and hints at the secrecy within Jekyll's domain. According to Alexander Gourlay, 'baize is a kind of felt that is best-known nowadays as a fabric on billiard tables'. However, 'in the eighteenth century it was also used as a covering for certain doors, specifically the traditional 'green baize door' that separated the domain of servants from public areas of any house grand enough to support the distinction'.[31] In this sense, the 'red baize' may reflect the boundary between the public face of Jekyll and his private one. As 'baize' covers what is underneath, it could also represent how the true nature of man is kept out of sight and locked behind a door.

The 'red', used to describe the baize, symbolises danger, a warning signal that entering this zone will have terrible consequences. 'Red' also has connotations of desire, perhaps reflecting how behind this door is a space where Jekyll's repressed desires can roam freely.

This chapter highlights the fraught relationship between the upper and lower classes. Poole has to visit Utterson in order to prompt him finally to 'come along [...] and see for [himself]'. Back at Jekyll's house, the

---

[31] Alexander Gourlay, 'The Red Baize Door in The Strange Case of Dr. Jekyll and Mr. Hyde,' *Notes and Queries*, Volume 60 (2) – Jun 5, 2013, (p. 273).

servants are described as standing 'huddled together like a flock of sheep'. The simile portrays them as frightened and vulnerable, like the prey of Hyde, but also suggests that are lost, unable to act or think for themselves without some sort of leader.

Despite their not unreasonable fear, Utterson scolds the servants, treating them like children, stating that their actions are 'very irregular, very unseemly' and telling them sternly that their 'master would be far from pleased'. This reflects how the professional classes happily imposed their authority upon those below them and the way Utterson refers to Jekyll as 'master' reinforces class boundaries. Utterson's promptness to think about how the scene at Jekyll's house might be  seen by others ['unseemly'], i.e. his obvious concern for his friend's reputation, again suggests the fundamental inappropriateness of his role as detective on this 'case'. Utterson is actually keener to cover things up than to uncover them – his prime aim seems to be to avoid exposing a gentleman's shame to the public. Why, for example, hasn't he called the police? Poole notes that Jekyll, or 'whatever it is', could be heard 'crying night and day for some sort of medicine' and adds that it is 'wanted bitter bad'. The emasculating verb 'crying' highlights Jekyll's desperation and intense craving for the drug. This brings another reading of the protagonist into focus. We have already seen that Hyde is the embodiment of what Victorians would call a degenerate. Perhaps Jekyll represents the nineteenth century drug addict with Hyde the wild other self, liberated by drugs. Indeed there was a growing discourse about addiction and drugs in the period. As Patricia Comitini points out:

'Doctors in the late nineteenth century occupied a unique position, being among the few qualified professionals to prescribe and dispense opium and its alkaloids, as well as

---

to experiment with forms of coca [...] Even early in the nineteenth century, there was no real distinction between the medicinal and what we would now call the recreational use of opium.'[32]

If we adopt this reading of Jekyll and Hyde as embodying the nineteenth century drug addict, it explains why Jekyll so rapidly loses control over Hyde. The grip of addiction tightens over time as Jekyll moves from wanting it 'bitter bad' to using blasphemous, assertive language, 'For God's sake, find some'. Also, the characters in the novella are both attracted to as well as repelled by Hyde, reflecting a wider recognition of the temptation of drug-taking, especially as an escape from the oppressive conventions of Victorian social norms.

In this chapter, Poole also details his encounter with Hyde. This provides the reader with another account, this time from the perspective of a character from a different strata of society. Poole refers to 'a kind of cry', portraying Hyde as child-like and says that Hyde has 'a mask upon his face', recalling the idea of Victorian gentlemen leading a double life. What is more, Poole likens Hyde to a 'rat,' associating him with vermin and the spreading of plague. Perhaps, this implies fear that Hyde might infect society with his own moral disease. Poole cannot believe the figure he's seen, a 'dwarf', could possibly be his master and comes to the conclusion that this figure may have murdered Jekyll.

As the chapter progresses, Utterson seems to become more involved, and he refers to it as his 'duty to make certain' by 'break[ing] in that

---

[32] Patricia Comitini, 'The Strange Case of Addiction in Robert Louis Stevenson's Strange Case of Dr. Jekyll and Mr. Hyde,' *Victorian Review*, Spring 2012, Vol. 38, No. 1 (Spring 2012), pp. 113-131 (p. 116).

door'. Poole's response is telling in that it exposes the difference between them. Poole has to seek permission to break in and Utterson reassures him that he will not suffer as a consequence. Though they work together here, Poole is the one that actually 'swung the axe,' hinting perhaps that the Victorian gentleman does not have the same capacity to take decisive physical action as his social inferior. Indeed, Stevenson may be suggesting that it is the lower echelons of society that seem, in some ways, more advanced, as Poole demonstrates an ability to take action, unlike Utterson who can only declare, 'This is beyond me, Poole'.

The moment when Poole swings the axe is a pivotal point in the novella. The narrator states: 'the blow shook the building, and the red baize door leaped against the lock and hinges'.

Obviously a door prevents entry and acts as a physical barrier. Poole's removal of it releases the secrets contained within and expose to the world the double life of a Victorian gentleman. The plosive 'blow' and the verb 'shook' signal the disorder Victorian society will now have to suffer, as it is forced to confront the dark secrets that lie within. The breakdown of the 'lock' signals that keeping secrets is not a long-term solution and that they cannot be contained forever. Rather, Stevenson suggests that secrets must be negotiated and acknowledged, sooner rather than later, if one is to avoid a path to self-destruction.

This chapter is also key in highlighting the consequences of the burdens that Jekyll and Hyde carried together. Within the room, Utterson and Poole locate 'the body of a man sorely contorted and still twitching'. Jekyll it seems was unable to achieve peace, even when approaching death. He is labelled as a suicide, 'a self-destroyer', as 'the strong smell of kernels [...] hung upon the air'. Perhaps, Jekyll took cyanide, as there was no other route that he could take to escape his plight. However, what has led him on this path has been a toxic combination of obsession with science and the oppressive pressure of Victorian social mores.

Stevenson is also offering a universal message about mental health that resonates in our current social context. No one realised that Jekyll was so unhappy, because they assumed that high status and material possessions must bring happiness.

In keeping with the Gothic genre, the narrative form alters and Stevenson switches to an epistolary mode. This enables the reader to experience the thoughts and feelings of Jekyll from his own voice, rather than having them filtered through the voices of other characters. It is no coincidence that the chapter ends on a note of secrecy once more. Despite what Utterson has experienced, he is portrayed as someone who seems fixated on maintaining reputations, even if this involves burying the truth. Though he tells Poole that he can 'foresee that [they] may yet involve [his] master in some dire catastrophe', he instructs him to keep quiet, to saying 'nothing' about the letter. Utterson is most concerned to ensure that they 'may at least save' Jekyll' 'credit' a word that conflates reputation with money in a bank. Although Utterson does seem totally fixated on status and reputation, Stevenson is equally positioning him as a victim. The lawyer cannot see beyond the social conventions that compromise his integrity.

The way that the chapter ends with Utterson and Poole 'locking the door of the theatre' is significant. Perhaps, the way they both leave together indicates a new sense of acceptance between them. Alternatively, relocking the cabinet may also represent the idea of containment - locking the door so that the secrets of Jekyll remain within. Perhaps Utterson and Poole's movement away from the theatre has even greater significance, as Douglas S. Mack opines:

> Jekyll's scientific experiments, which advance knowledge but also release evil, are conducted in a laboratory that had formerly been a dissecting theatre; and this calls to mind the Edinburgh dissecting theatre of Dr. Robert Knox. Knox's work as a dissector advanced scientific knowledge; but it also released evil through the activities of Burke and Hare, who began to murder tramps and prostitutes in order to keep up their lucrative trade in supplying dead bodies to Dr. Knox.[33]

---

[33] Douglas S. Mack, 'Scottish Gothic,' in *The Handbook of Gothic Literature*, ed. by Marie Mulbey-Roberts, (Basingstoke: Macmillan Press, 1998), pp. 208-210 (p. 210).

# Chapter Nine: Dr. Lanyon's Narrative

This chapter is crucial in that it finally establishes that Jekyll and Hyde are inextricably linked, in a brilliant twist revealing that they are, in fact, two halves of the same person. Written from Lanyon's point of view, this chapter features one of the most extended first-person accounts to appear in the novella. Structurally it is significant that as we reach the end of the chapter, more extended details are provided, as it signals the release of the secrets that have been kept under lock and key in Jekyll's cabinet for such a long time. This chapter is also instrumental in terms of revealing that Hyde by 'Jekyll's own confession [...] [was] the murderer of Carew'. By positioning this revelation at the end of the novel enables, as Benjamin O'Dell notes finally exposes 'the red herring of Jekyll's criminal desires'.[34]

From the outset, this chapter portrays tension between the two scientists. The chapter begins with the epistolary narrative from. Here Jekyll adopts a much more manipulative and persuasive approach, highlighted through the imperative language when he tells Lanyon 'to drive to my house'. At the end of the letter, Jekyll writes, 'serve me, my dear Lanyon'. Earlier in the novella Jekyll had referred to Lanyon as a 'hide-bound pedant', so clearly things have now changed. In fact, in his desperation for release, Jekyll is using Lanyon and the latter will suffer as a consequence.

---

[34] Benjamin D. O'Dell, 'Character Crisis: Hegemonic Negotiations in Robert Louis Stevenson's *The Strange Case of Dr. Jekyll and Mr. Hyde*,' *Victorian Literature and Culture*. 2012. Vol. 40, No. 2 (2012), pp. 509-521 (p. 511).

In this letter, the cabinet is again mentioned, and Jekyll states that the 'door of my cabinet' must be 'forced'. Forcing something open indicates that Lanyon will be entering a situation that is perhaps better left alone. It also reflects Stevenson's view that tapping into forbidden knowledge can bring danger and destruction.

The reader is also given an insight to how Lanyon thinks and feels about Jekyll. Instantly, he believes'[his] colleague was insane' and the professional address 'colleague' demonstrates that there is little room for friendship. Lanyon is simply supporting Jekyll for the sake of his conscience, especially as he 'felt bound to do as [Jekyll] requested'. Alternatively, Lanyon's gradual involvement with Jekyll here may also highlight the tempting nature of the unknown, as the very rigid views of Lanyon are clearly not enough to prevent him from becoming involved with Jekyll's experimental science.

Lanyon diagnoses Jekyll 'with a case of cerebral disease'. Trying to apply established scientific notions, like Utterson, Lanyon struggles to comprehend and categories Jekyll's apparent irrationality. Though Lanyon and Jekyll may be connected by profession, their understanding of the world are far apart.

 The chemicals within Jekyll's chamber are ominous. There is 'a simple crystalline salt of white colour' and 'a blood-red liquor,' signalling the sinister and destructive nature of Jekyll's experiments, as well as the unstoppable evil at play. The compound adjective 'blood-red' may also represent the idea that Jekyll's experiment will result in the blood he will have on his hands. It will not only be his own, but also those that are caught up in his uncivilised nature.

In addition, Lanyon provides a detailed description of Hyde's appearance. He describes Hyde as a 'distasteful curiosity' - as with other characters in the novella, the use of oxymoronic language demonstrates a sense of attraction as well as hatred. Hyde's clothes 'would have made an ordinary person laughable' as they were 'enormously too large for him in every measurement'. If we interpret Hyde as an embodiment of fears of the working-class during the

nineteenth century, then Lanyon's remarks suggest that Hyde's diminutive stature may be a result of poverty and malnourishment. Often the lower classes were regarded as less advanced and even as bestial, while the upper classes were considered to be more civilised. Hence part of Lanyon's feelings of revulsion towards Hyde may stem from the demonisation of the lower classes.

Stevenson is echoing the concerns of other Victorian writers, such as Dickens, who in *Great Expectations*, uses the character of Joe Gargery, the blacksmith to expose similar snobbery.

In this chapter, we are also provided with an account of Hyde's transformation. As noted earlier, the adjective 'red' is used repeatedly, foreshadowing the destruction and blood that is about to be spilt due to Jekyll's hubris. The mixture has a 'reddish hue' but then transforms from red to 'a dark purple' and finally to a 'watery green'. Perhaps these three colours symbolize the different layer of man, the bestial, the socially constructed and the civilized. The mixture is liquid, moves freely and is interchangeable. Hence it could be a symbol of the similar fluidity of human identity drinking it unleashes.

At the end of the chapter, the clash between Lanyon and Jekyll becomes even more apparent. Earlier, Lanyon had condemned

'Jekyll's investigations [as they have] no practical usefulness'. This is ironic as what he witnesses here will cause Lanyon to re-evaluate his understanding of the nature of human identity. Jekyll tells him that he should remember 'the seal of our profession'. 'Seal' and the inclusive pronoun 'our' creates the idea of this as a shared, sacred promise that should never be broken. Yet, the plosive 'bound' and the noun phrase 'the most narrow and material views' indicate that Hyde/Jekyll regards him as a potential hinderance to scientific development, as Lanyon has denied 'the virtue of transcendental medicine'. Furthermore, Hyde/Jekyll asserts his dominance over Lanyon in this chapter, and perhaps this clash between them reflects the wider scientific debate taking place in the context of the late nineteenth century. Hyde/Jekyll refers to himself as part of the 'superiors', placing Lanyon as below him, and as unworthy of being labelled as a true scientist.

The description of Hyde's transformation is an extraordinary powerful piece of writing. The asyndetic list of 'reeled, staggered, clutched' provides both a picture of Hyde's sudden, jerky movements and conveys his desperation. We are given quick close-ups of 'injected eyes' and a 'gasping' 'open mouth'. Then Hyde's body seems to 'swell'. His face becomes suddenly 'black' before, most horribly it seems, like wax, to dissolve and 'melt'.

Unsurprisingly, Lanyon is unable to cope with the visceral, uncanny, deeply unsettling experience of witnessing Hyde's transformation back into Jekyll. The syndetic listing 'I saw what I saw, I heard what I heard, and my soul sickened' demonstrates that every aspect of the transformation has affected him to his core. 'Soul sickened' also suggests that Lanyon feels contaminated and corrupted, and this could demonstrate the idea that unleashing the unknown can be toxic and destructive.

---

Perhaps, like the rest of the characters in the novella, he feels such sickness and repulsion in part because it reminds him of what he has tried to ignore about others and about himself, that even apparently good men like Jekyll, like Utterson, like himself, may contain a monstrous Hyde somewhere buried within them.

Most significantly of all, perhaps, Hyde/Jekyll is portrayed as satanic. Like Adam and Eve, who were tempted to acquire the forbidden fruit, Stevenson presents science and the acquisition of knowledge as the forbidden fruit for Jekyll and Lanyon. In this sense, as Adam and Eve were expelled from the Garden of Eden, Jekyll and Lanyon's punishment for falling victim to temptation is banishment from society and eventually death. As Benjamin O'Dell opines *The Strange Case of Dr. Jekyll and Mr. Hyde* is so frightening because it dramatizes what happens when the fundamental boundaries on which life depends are undermined And challenged.[35] What can be more fundamental to our understanding of the world around us than the boundary between ourselves and others? What can be more fundamental to our sense of ourselves than the fact that we are one person and not two? Hyde's transformation into Jekyll and Jekyll's back into Hyde bends and finally undermines both of these fundamental laws of reality.

---

[35] Benjamin D. O'Dell, p. 519.

# Chapter Ten: Henry Jekyll's Full Statement of the Case

This chapter fulfils its title; it does exactly what it says on the tin. We'll discuss exactly how Jekyll is presented in chapter ten in our essay on him as a character. So, we will cover the material only briefly for now.

In this chapter Stevenson's switches narrators, so that for the first time Jekyll tells his own story. What follows is a re-run of events we've witnessed before, but this time we're on the inside track. In effect, Jekyll puts the flesh on the bones of the story and confirms details we have only gleaned previously second-hand through the experiences of other characters.

We learn in this chapter that Jekyll was born into money, was highly ambitious and craved the good esteem of his peers. But he was plagued by a feeling that his self was split, that underneath his grave, eminent public self was another more selfish self, which craved only 'undignified pleasures'. Hence he started to lead a double life.

The intolerable pressure of containing these two violently opposing impulses and the fear that his baser self might bring shame upon his better half, Jekyll began to conduct experiments with a view to splitting the two selves apart, thus releasing the good from the bad. Initially he was exultant at the results. The potion he concocted released him to satisfy his ungentlemanly appetites, whatever these may have been, without fear that this base behaviour would ruin the reputation of the good doctor.

However, this exuberance soon gave way to anxiety and then to despair. The more Jekyll indulged his Hyde self, the more powerful Hyde became, and the more difficult it became to suppress him. Worse, Jekyll discovered that as time went on he was turning into Hyde without the catalyst of taking the drugs.

A mortal battle ensues. Jekyll redoubles his efforts to live a good life and to keep his Hyde self locked firmly away. Realising, however, that he cannot control Hyde forever, he makes preparations to defeat him in the only way possible, trying desperately to avoid Hyde detecting his plans. Finally Jekyll understands that the only way to kill Hyde is to poison himself.

The tone of this chapter is confessional. Jekyll is finally revealing the secrets he has kept locked within his chest and in his laboratory for so long. If we remember that Utterson and Poole seem to discover Hyde, not Jekyll, dead in the laboratory, it seems that Jekyll acted just in time.

Why didn't Stevenson add another chapter at the end of the novella? What might Utterson do with this confession? Will he hand it over to the police? Will, finally, all the novella's locked doors be opened and the hidden secrets exposed to the glare of public opinion? Or will he burn it? We'll never know. And that's why Stevenson leaves the ending open in this tantalizing way.

# Settings

Typically in the first wave of the Gothic, beginning in the late eighteenth-century, novels were set in faraway places, faraway both in the sense of geography and time. Most commonly Gothic novels were set in southern European locations, such as Italy or Spain, and the events they depicted took place in some unspecified period in the past. For the protestant English writers and their readers these locations were associated with hot-blooded irrationality and often with Catholicism. Though reading one of the first Gothic novels may have been thrilling in the way a ghost-train ride at a theme park might be thrilling, the reader could feel safe in the knowledge that any danger the novels contained was far removed from their own lives. That isn't the case with the second wave of Gothic novels which bring Gothic terror both into the present and onto the streets of England's capital city, London. And not only onto the streets, but into real places with familiar names and even into the interior, domestic, conventionally safe spaces of the home.

## Urban nightmares

At the time Stevenson was writing, London was home to around five million inhabitants and it was considerably the biggest and most populous city on earth. It was a centre of great power - the centre of the British Empire which stretched across almost half the globe - and, for the English at least, London was also the centre of human civilization. As well as being the august seat of the British government, London boasted some of the most cultured and prosperous suburbs on the planet. But it was also a city filled with terrible poverty, with infamous slums, with disease, destitution and social deprivation on a scale never seen before in England.

And these two Londons existed uneasily together in one city. The elite,

 wealthy, culturally sophisticated world, in which flourished writers such as Oscar Wilde, existed alongside the unbelievably harsh, dark and stunted worlds depicted in the work of writers such as Charles Dickens. Unsurprisingly, crime in all its various malign guises, was also rife in Victorian London - prostitution, drug dens, pickpockets, street gangs, violent robbery, murder.

During this period the phenomena of reverse colonization was another source of fear and anxiety. Britain had conquered half the globe and now some of these people were coming to the centre of the Empire to make new lives. Fear of the racial other jostled with fear of the working class other and the criminal other and the homosexual other within the increasingly fearful and gloomy Late Victorian psyche. Jekyll and Hyde is not only a portrait of a character, but the embodiment of Victorian London.

While the hustle and bustle of the city, its business, might be reassuring, in the Late Victorian period the urban itself became an object of fear and anxiety. As in Stevenson's novella, the city streets could be like a labyrinth, and, worse, fog or smog could descend making it even harder to navigate a safe route through.

There was also something anonymous too about the city; people didn't know you and you didn't know them, so the bonds of obligation that knit people together were loosened. As Hyde, Jekyll expresses exactly this sentiment and revels in the freedom, the freedom to do harm. Fear of the anonymous stranger and of the unfortunate chance encounter with them grew. Think of the poor girl in the novella who just happens to be coming around a corner as Hyde is coming like a 'juggernaut' towards her or the random collision of Danvers Carew and Hyde. Stevenson ups the ante of anxiety further, because in his novella this dangerous stranger might look as benign, respectable and unthreatening as the eminent Dr. Henry Jekyll. Who would have thought that such a gentleman could be so very dangerous?

Stevenson's protagonist also encapsulates another duality in Fin-De-Siecle Britain, that between public virtue and private vice. Public discourse in Victorian culture was characterised by its high moral tone and piety. Late Victorian gentlemen were expected to conform to strict codes of conduct and present themselves with the stiff moral sobriety fitting to their station in life. Sex was not to be discussed in polite society. Etiquette and propriety were everything. But underneath this cover of polite respectability was a very different world of crime and vice, of temptation, sin and punishment.

Perhaps Stevenson's London is based on Edinburgh, but his use of actual place names, such as Soho, relocate the Gothic in the real, familiar world around the reader and make reading his novella a much more intimately unsettling experience.

## Utterson's London

In the novella's first chapter Utterson and Enfield are off on one of their habitual rambles through London when they find themselves wandering down a by-street in a 'busy quarter' of the city. Though small, the street they chance upon is 'thriving' with trade and its enterprising inhabitants have laid out the 'surplus of their grains in coquetry' on their shop fronts. 'Coquetry' seems an unusual choice of word here, as it carries the sense of sexual flirtatiousness. We might wonder what the street's more 'florid charms' are exactly and whether this phrase is a polite euphemism for 'charms' that are now covered-up, 'veiled', by the sombreness of a Victorian Sunday. Already there are hints of impropriety and perhaps illicit and hidden attractions.

This bright, busy street 'shone out in contrast to its dingy neighbourhood, like a fire in a forest'. So the street is situated in a gloomy, 'dismal' area, which we later discover is the notorious London district of Soho, and we may reasonably also wonder what Utterson and Enfield are doing entering this infamously disreputable quarter. What exactly 'led them **down**' this way? 'Fire' obviously suggests there is some danger here, while the comparison to a forest reverses the normal associations of a city and connects this location to wild spaces, places in which it is easy to get lost, both in the literal and metaphorical sense.

The street is like a light in the dark, attractive to moths. And only 'two doors from one corner' there is darkness within this light, a 'certain sinister block of building thrust forward' onto the street. This sinister building, which is marked by 'prolonged and sordid negligence', is windowless. Nobody can see out of it and nobody can see into it. Strikingly, Stevenson describes the 'discoloured' upper story as like a 'blind forehead'. In short, this building has the physiognomy of a Victorian degenerate and, more specifically, of a primitive criminal type. It is the outer manifestation of its secret inhabitant, Mr. Hyde.

We learn later than a secret passage links this building to Jekyll's handsome house nearby. Jekyll's home is the inverse of Hyde's. Set within a square of houses that have become 'decayed from their high estate' and are now sublet and occupied by all sorts of disreputable, shady characters, Jekyll's house is still 'occupied entire'. Its door 'wore a great air of wealth and comfort', though when Utterson arrives at this door it is ominously 'plunged in darkness'. 'Wore', of course, is a verb with many resonances in this story. Clearly both these houses, both located two doors from a corner, mirror their occupants, as does the secret link between them.

There is a door too at Hyde's house. This door has no 'bell or knocker' [unlike the one in our image] with which to communicate with its

 inhabitant. The door is also 'blistered' as if it is skin, skin suffering some sort of infection, and 'distained', a verb suggestive of sin and carrying the echo of 'distained', a verb commonly applied to negative feelings about a person. Around the ravaged door the destitute and desperate while away their time. This door has a peculiar story attached to it and we discover that Enfield has 'studied the place' for himself. Nevertheless, after hearing the story the two friends decide to stick to Enfield's convenient maxim, 'the more it looks like Queer Street, the less I ask'.

However, the despicable story of Hyde is not so easily dropped by the lawyer. It haunts and grips his imagination. Soon he finds himself dreaming of the 'great field of lamps of a nocturnal city' and of random collisions within the 'wider labyrinths' of a 'lamplighted city' leading inexorably to a child's screams. Soon he is stumping these lamplit, solitary streets at night, looking for Hyde. Around his solitary figure, like some sort of predatory animal or beast, London emits a 'low growl'. As he travels in a carriage through fog that is like a funeral 'pall' obscuring 'heaven', Utterson enters an eerie twilight zone. For Utterson, London, or more specifically this area of it, is becoming a Gothic liminal space, like a 'district of some city in a nightmare'.

# Characters

## Dr. Jekyll

Throughout the novella, characters have described Dr. Jekyll for us through their perspective. We are also offered glimpses of him - entertaining friends, sitting at a window and heard snatches of his conversations. But it isn't until the final chapter of Stevenson's book that we are given any extended access to him as a character.

The final chapter re-tells the whole story, but this time from the privileged, insider view of the first-person perspective of both its protagonist and antagonist. And this perspective is able to fill in some pieces of the puzzle that have eluded Utterson and his associates.

We learn that Jekyll is wealthy, having been born into a 'large fortune' and that he was also unusually lucky in the lottery of life, having been 'endowed besides with excellent parts', if he does say so himself. But, from early in his life, Jekyll was deeply conflicted. Though he had an 'imperious desire' to 'carry his head high' and to 'wear a more than commonly grave countenance' this was undermined by a natural 'gaiety of disposition'. The result was a split in his self between public virtue and private vice so that, over time, he became a 'profound double dealer'.

Hence Jekyll's obsession with finding a way to cut the two halves of himself asunder and in so doing to save his good half from his bad. Initially he experiences the transformation into Hyde as a kind of wild, exuberant liberation. He 'plunged' into it, like diving into a swimming pool and 'sprung headlong' into a vast 'sea of liberty'. For such an emotionally repressed Victorian gentleman, plunging and springing into a vast 'sea' must have been exhilarating. As Hyde, he felt more

vigorous - 'younger, lighter' and even 'happier'. The sensation of being Hyde, able to indulge his appetites, 'delighted' him 'like wine'. In other words, he was intoxicated by the freedom from social responsibilities and by the epic widening of opportunity to do as he pleased. In addition, he could assuage his 'undignified pleasures', whatever these might be, without facing any consequences, even when these pleasures 'began to turn toward', began to become a 'monstrous depravity'.

Jekyll is one of several upper middle-class gentlemen living a life of 'profound duplicity' in Late Victorian literature. Within the Gothic, for instance, he shares his appetite for the depraved with Oscar Wilde's angelic looking, unageing Dorian Gray. But Jekyll is also a Gothic cousin of the male characters in Wilde's plays, such as Algernon and Jack in *The Importance of Being Earnest* who behave one way in the city and a distinctly different way when they are in the country. Indeed, Algernon even invents a term, 'Bunburying', to describe indulging in a secret second life.

What was it about Victorian gentleman that led to them living the sort of double existence depicted by Stevenson and Wilde? Certainly the strictness of a social code that demanded graveness, earnestness and moral sobriety at all time in Victorian gentlemen played a part. As their stiff, formal clothes suggest, Victorian middle-class were also very buttoned up, both in the physical sense and also the emotional. Men were not expected to show their emotions, especially not if these emotions might betray weakness of any kind. Hence men's emotions were commonly repressed.

Additionally, Victorian ladies were idealized as 'angels of the house' - sexless, perfect, almost ethereal beings. If sexual relations within the home were no longer desirable or possible, Victorian men had to seek elsewhere for gratification of these needs. And that took them into the more dubious, seedier areas of London. Many social historians have noted the proliferation of prostitution in Late Victorian London, despite the high mora, often pious tone and the sexual prudery of the public culture. This is the sort of situation that led to Jekyll linking indulging in pleasure with feeling terribly ashamed of himself.

Perhaps too characters like Jekyll/Hyde embody eternal tensions, tensions within Victorian society, but also within every society and, indeed, within each of us. Jekyll embodies the social self, linked to other people and wider society by a network of relationships and responsibilities. As a doctor he tries selflessly to help the needy and reduce human suffering. But within him is another more individualistic self, a self not interested at all in social relations or other people. Hyde embodies the rampantly egotistical self, the self only concerned with appeasing its own appetites, hungry and thirsty for pleasure, monstrously greedy and destructive, deaf to the suffering of others.

Perhaps the most interesting thing about Jekyll is the question who exactly is Jekyll? The speaker of the final chapter defines himself in various, often contradictory ways, calling himself both Jekyll and Hyde and yet also somehow uncannily separating himself from both, as if both are merely personas adopted by a separate consciousness. At times, this speaker dissociates himself from his own actions and at other times he owns them. We have, for example, already quoted the line where the narrator says he felt 'younger, lighter, happier' as Hyde. Here he uses the first-person singular pronoun – 'I felt younger'. So, in this instance he *is* Hyde. However, at other times the speaker refers to Hyde in the third person. For instance, he says that when Hyde escaped after a long confinement while Jekyll tried to suppress his appetites, 'my devil had so long been caged **he** came out roaring'. A few lines later, however, the narration slips back again into first-person: 'the spirit of hell awoke in **me** and raged'. When he finds himself changing without the drugs, the speaker says, '**I** was once more Mr. Hyde'. Most disturbingly, when he recounts the killing of Sir Carew Danvers the narrator admits that '**I** mauled the unresisting body'.

As the title of the chapter refer to Henry Jekyll's 'full statement' we reasonably expect the narration to be from Jekyll's perspective. But, as with Hyde, at times, Jekyll also seems to be no more than a persona or even a theatrical costume that the narrator assumes whenever it suits him. Referring to drinking the potion, for instance, he says that he only had to 'drink the cup' and he could 'doff the body of the noted professor'. Putting on his Hyde self is also presented as stepping into a costume, as like putting on a 'thick cloak'. Elsewhere this mysterious not quite Jekyll, not quite Hyde narrator refers to being able to 'shrug off these lendings' – note the plural – and choosing to 'wear the countenance of Jekyll' – note the third person. He refers to preferring the 'elderly and discontented doctor', as if this doctor was someone else, just an associate. This liminal consciousness also says that 'Jekyll was now my city of refuge', again suggesting his true self is hiding within a shell-like persona.

Arguably, all these confusing references to I, he, Jekyll and Hyde are the inevitable result of Stevenson's brilliant central conceit of making the two characters, protagonist and antagonist, one character. On the other hand, perhaps what we see almost revealed, but still half concealed, is this character's true inner self, an 'independent denizen' who is neither quite entirely Jekyll nor entirely Hyde.

# Mr. Hyde

In Gothic novels of the first wave, starting in the late eighteenth century, the narrative perspective concentrated on the virtuous heroine and not on her cruel persecutor. One of the major ways in which Mary Shelley innovated within the genre in *Frankenstein* [1818] was that she gave the creature both a voice and a psychological depth previous villains had lacked, with a whole middle section of the novel narrated from the creature's point of view. Like Hyde, the creature is also not merely supernatural and hence created by some sort of mysterious metaphysical forces, but is created through science. Shelley may also have given Stevenson the idea of the doppelganger as the creature can be read as representing the suppressed aspects of Victor Frankenstein's psyche.

As we have already established in our chapter summaries, Hyde is a mysterious amalgam of various Late Victorian fears, anxieties and hidden desires. In particular, he can be interpreted as embodying fears of a variety of people Late Victorian culture labelled as degenerate. He can be read as representing homosexuality or the working or the criminal classes, for instance. He is also a degenerate in the sense that he appears to be some kind of evolutionary throwback, a neandertal, ape-like and 'troglodytic'. If we read the novella as being about Scotland and the Scottish psyche specifically, this atavism has even be interpreted as embodying the fear of the enduring influence of the

Celtic in the protestant imagination.

In addition, the distinguished and respectable Dr. Jekyll is transformed into the repellent Hyde through the taking of a drug; hence Jekyll/Hyde can also be interpreted as Stevenson's depiction of a degenerate drug addict. Another possible reading focuses on how Hyde appears to be much younger that Jekyll and occasional suggestions in the novella that their relationship is akin to a father and son. In which case the characters represent intergenerational tensions and fears of fathers that their sons might be become sort of terrible progeny.

The fact that none of the characters is able to describe Hyde's appearance with any precision indicates that he can also embody urban fears of anonymous strangers anybody could happen to come across in the labyrinthine streets of a city where the poor and the rich lived cheek by jowl. As we've also noted, the difficulty characters have in describing Hyde's exact physical appearance implies that degeneracy might be more difficult to spot than degeneration theory had suggested. How much more menacing and dangerous would degeneracy be, Stevenson implies, if it is an invisible threat?

Clearly Stevenson's novella is responding to fears sparked by Darwin's theory of evolution that, given the right or perhaps the wrong circumstances, human beings might regress into more savage and primitive states. Like *Frankenstein*, the novella also expresses fears about science itself as an enterprise, specifically what rogue, unregulated scientific experiments might reveal or create as mankind pushes back ever further the boundaries of knowledge.

Finally, Stevenson's novella is also influenced by the thinking of another branch of science, the newly emerging discipline of psychology. The fin-de-siecle was the period during which the father of modern psychology, Sigmund Freud, was developing his theories about the inner workings of the human mind.

Two of Freud's revelations were particularly unsettling and are pertinent to Stevenson's work. Firstly, Freud claimed that half of what constitutes our identity is hidden from us and resides in our subconscious. Only from time to time, such as in our dreams, do we have any access to this other self that drives our behaviour, according to Freud, just as much as our waking, rational selves. In other words, human behaviour, the decisions we make, the things we do, our fears and desires, is driven by forces invisible to the rational mind. In essence, we are alienated from our own selves. Within us dwells another self, a stranger just as much in charge of things as the person we know ourselves to be. Secondly, Freud opined that our minds are split into different aspects and that these are constantly in conflict with themselves. Freud labelled these aspects the Id, Ego and the Superego.

If you imagine a darts board, the Id is the bulls eye in the centre. The Id is the innermost, ancient core of our minds, the animalistic self that governs instincts, our fears and desires, our fight or flight instinct. Around this, like the numbers round the bulls eye, is the Ego, by which Freud means the rational aspect of our mind; our capacity to hypothecate, to draw conclusions, and to understand consequences. The final layer of self is the like the black surround of the darts board. This is the Superego, which Freud defines as the internalized rules and values of whatever culture we live in. The Superego is the thinnest layer and on the outside because it is the most liable to change. If we move into a new culture, over time we are likely to internalize a slightly different set of values.

The conflict in the mind is a battle between the powers of the wild Id and the controlling and policing forces of the Ego and Superego. Think, for instance, if you have a real craving and hunger for chocolate and you want to eat loads of it because it tastes delicious. That is your Id talking. But really you know that if you eat lots and lots of chocolate you will eventually feel sick and over time you're also likely to put on weight and your complexion might suffer, so you'd be wise to restrain yourself. That is your sensible Ego and Superego talking in unison.

Read through a psychological prism, Hyde is an emanation of the Id and Jekyll represents the Ego and Superego trying to contain it. But, why are this version of the Id's desires so sordid, destructive and violent? Perhaps it is because Victorian gentlemen were so emotionally repressed and so tightly bound by strict social conventions of sobriety and moral earnestness that they were not able to release their desires and fears in more healthy ways. The suppression of perfectly natural desires and fears leads, according to Freud, to them festering and fermenting, corrupting within the psyche, and the harder these feelings are pushed and held down, the harder they will spring out once released. Think of a lid of a pan full of vigorously bowling water or a monkey rattling the bars of its cage. Perhaps the most disturbing way to think about Hyde is in these psychological terms, as the stranger within all of us, as the self as the dangerous, unknown other.

# Utterson

By profession Utterson is a lawyer. He is therefore fundamentally concerned with upholding law and order. As an upper middle-class, middle-aged male, he is also a member of a ruling elite, an educated class of men that governed Victorian society. By nature he is sober, serious and conventional in his habits. Not much prone to extravagant flights of fancy, he appears to be a solid and dependable type, the sort of character who will do things by the book and with steady determination. His personality seems well-suited to the narrative role of trustworthy confidant to his fellow upper-middle class male friends, Jekyll, Lanyon and Enfield. Utterson's the sort of solid chap one might turn to in a pickle, someone who will provide good, sensible, robust advice.

As a character type Utterson also seems well-fitted to the role of the novella's detective. Maybe not the Sherlock Holmes type of detective with a sparklingly brilliant intellect and leaps of dazzling insight, but a more down-to-earth, dogged sort of detective, one who follows the correct procedures and examines evidence with logical and systematic thoroughness. Why then, if he's constitutionally well-suited to the role, does Utterson do such a poor job of investigating this particular case? Why does he not alert the police to the blackmail plot he suspects has ensnared his friend, Dr. Jekyll? Why does he not call the police when he thinks Hyde is planning to murder Jekyll? Why, after the brutal killing of Sir Danvers Carew does he allow a murderer to apparently vanish without facing justice? And why does he act too slowly to save Jekyll from his awful fate? Why? Why? Why?

Indeed, Utterson seems rather reluctant to pick up the role of the story's detective. When he is initially told the story of Mr. Hyde's battering of an innocent young girl, he agrees heartily with Enfield's conclusion that 'here is another lesson to say nothing'. The friends then agree to 'never refer' to the story again and shake hands on a pact. Utterson agrees to this pact of silence, fervently, with all his heart.

However, when Utterson gets home that evening, he opens his safe to peruse the will of Dr. Jekyll. The will's beneficiary is, of course, Mr. Edward Hyde. Now it is not so easy for Utterson to do nothing. Now it isn't just some young street girl who has been hurt; it appears that one of his gentleman friends is imperilled.

As the story unfolds, Utterson seems to hover awkwardly between wanting to uncover the truth, particularly as it pertains to Mr. Hyde and to cover it up, particularly in terms of its potential damage to the reputation of Dr. Jekyll. Not only is Utterson a partial and unreliable narrator, but he's also a partial, unreliable investigator.

Maybe it isn't only Jekyll's reputation that Utterson seeks to protect. What we wonder is the true nature of austere Utterson's friendship with the 'well-known man about town' Enfield? The narration tells us that 'it was a nut to crack for many, what these two could see in each other'. Puzzlingly, when others chance upon this odd couple on their regular excursions through London, they find them to be silent and looking so 'singularly dull' that they are relieved by the 'appearance of a friend'. Yet, curiously, Utterson and Enfield apparently viewed their rambles as the 'chief jewel of each week', setting work and other pleasures aside to ensure they could continue 'uninterrupted'.

If you think we're making a mountain of a molehill, isn't it rather odd that these two respectable gentlemen choose to visit a particular street in Soho, a district notorious for its links with crime and the sex industry?

We comment on the rather suggestive details in the description of this location elsewhere in this critical guide, so there's no need to go over them again now. But surely we must wonder why Utterson and Enfield are drawn to this street with its semi-hidden 'florid charms'. We might bear in mind the fact that Victorian dens of iniquity were often hidden behind seemingly innocuous facades and that Victorian prudery led to a coded, symbolic language used for taboo topics, such as sex.

As we also discuss in our themes section, Utterson's rather inept and sometimes half-hearted investigation of the case mirrors the Victorian police and judiciary's investigation of what has become known as the Cleveland Street Scandal. When eminent Victorian men, members of the establishment elite, were implicated in this sex-for-sale scandal, there seems to have been something of an establishment cover-up. Possibly tipped off that arrest was imminent, one of the accused, a well-known lord of the realm, fled to France and no less a figure than the Lord Chancellor blocked prosecution. Later the Prime Minister of the day ensured that attempts to extradite the Lord were quietly dropped.

Perhaps, then, Utterson is an adequate investigator not just due to his loyalty to Jekyll and his desire to protect his friend's reputation, but also because he is, in some unnamed way, himself compromised.

# Lanyon

Dr. Lanyon's main roles in the novella are as trusted confidante for Utterson and as a foil for Jekyll. Utterson sees his friend as a font of knowledge and seeks him out when he becomes troubled about Jekyll. If Jekyll represents the mad, hubristic scientist of the nineteenth century, then Lanyon represents a more rational-minded and conventional Victorian scientist, one who is sceptical about and disapproving of the transcendental nature of Jekyll's experiments.

Lanyon's house is located in a 'citadel of medicine', a detail that confirms his central place within the Victorian medical establishment. Clearly he is an eminent scientist; Utterson calls him 'the great Dr. Lanyon', suggesting both status and worldly renown. But Jekyll's experiments expose the limitations of Lanyon's more cautious and rigid scientific thinking. As well as not daring to investigate such territory, the rationalist Lanyon, like Utterson, seems also to lack the imagination to conceive such things might be possible. As with presenting the city itself as a site of degeneration, through Lanyon and his reaction to Jekyll's radicalism, Stevenson critiques the established thinking of Victorian science.

Lanyon doesn't just operate as a contrast to Jekyll, however. As is the case with Jekyll and the other male characters in the novella, there are hints that he too may be plagued by duality. In Chapter Two, he is described as 'a hearty, healthy, dapper, red-faced gentleman', but, like Utterson, Lanyon is forced to '[sit] alone over his wine', implying an inexplicably isolated existence.

Despite the gentlemanly exterior, Utterson notes a 'little spirit of temper' in Lanyon, a comment which echoes the 'slyish cast' of Jekyll.

Though his manner is youthful ['boisterous'] Lanyon's 'shock' of 'prematurely white hair' suggests something has aged him. In a novella where characters often seem to be performing roles, it seems significant that there is also something 'theatrical' about Lanyon's manner.

Stevenson also uses Lanyon as a tool for exposition, hinting at the nature of Jekyll's experiments. Despite their previous friendship, Lanyon is forthright in his hostility, even growing angry when he states that Jekyll 'became too fanciful [...] [and] began to go wrong, wrong in mind'. Perhaps, Lanyon's belief that Jekyll had become 'too fanciful' suggests he sensed Jekyll's experiment were pushing into hazardous and unethical terrain.

Structurally, Lanyon's character alters, as the once 'boisterous and decided manner' that he so openly displays is no longer evident later in the novella. In this sense, Lanyon follows the same trajectory as Jekyll, in that they both are broken by science, albeit Lanyon seems to be broken by what he witnesses of Jekyll's science. As one critic points out, 'Lanyon's and Jekyll's narratives follow immediately upon each other. Both are voices from the grave'.[36] It is significant that Stevenson keeps their narratives apart, as it reflects the detachment between them and that nothing can seem to bridge the gulf that has opened between them.

Nevertheless, for a short period of a couple of months Lanyon, Jekyll and Utterson socialize at Jekyll's and all seems to be well between a 'trio' who had once been 'inseparable friends'. Then, when Utterson is

---

[36] Irving S. Saposnik, 'The Anatomy of Dr. Jekyll and Mr. Hyde,' Studies in English Literature, 1500-1900 , Autumn, 1971, Vol. 11, No. 4, Nineteenth Century (Autumn, 1971), pp. 715-731 (p. 723).

denied admittance to Jekyll's house, he goes to Lanyon to seek explanations. The transformation he finds in Lanyon is extraordinary.

Now Lanyon is a 'doomed man' who has his 'death warrant written legibly on his face'. The aging process has been uncannily accelerated in him so that his 'rosy' complexion has become 'pale', his 'flesh' has 'fallen away' and he was 'visibly balder and older'. The outward deterioration reflects an inner one, with his manner now suggesting some kind of 'deep-seated terror of mind'. What, Utterson and the reader must think, can have happened to Lanyon to have transformed him like this?

If you were Stevenson, would you reveal the cause of Lanyon's change at this point in the novella? Or would you keep this mystery as another narrative hook to keep your reader reading? Of course, you'd keep the reader hooked. In fact, Stevenson increases the suspense when we discover a short while later that Lanyon has suddenly died. What killed a previously energetic and healthy middle-aged man? There are clues, of course, ones that seem more obvious when re-reading the novella. Lanyon's odd reaction to the mention of Jekyll and his reference to the 'accursed topic', for instance.

Paralleling Jekyll, Lanyon leaves a letter for Utterson to read. Like Jekyll, he also puts a prohibition on the letter being opened until after his death. More private letters, secrets and confessions - real and metaphorical locked doors and shameful things hidden behind them. Prohibitions, cover-ups and revelations. If Lanyon had allowed Utterson to read his account of visiting Jekyll in his laboratory perhaps the latter's death could have been avoided. A culture of cover-ups can have mortal consequences, the novella implies.

When eventually Utterson reads Lanyon's letter, for the first time the true nature of Jekyll's experiments is revealed, the transformation from Hyde to Jekyll is described and the novella's most brilliantly shocking twist is delivered - that Jekyll is Hyde.

Why does this miracle destroy Lanyon? There is, of course, the visceral horror of what he experiences. He finds Hyde disturbing and repulsive, then sees him drink the potion and Lanyon then witnesses first-hand the horrifically fluid metamorphosis into Jekyll. On top of that shock, the transformation undermines Lanyon's mind, because it breaks fundamental laws of science and of reality, as he understood them. What he witnesses also undermines the integrity of human identity. That's quite a double blow.

It is important to revisit Saposnik's assessment that 'Lanyon and Jekyll are voices from the grave.'[37] Indeed, Lanyon's demise is anticipated in Chapter Nine, as he says:

> 'My life is shaken to its roots; sleep has left me; the deadliest terror sits by me at all hours of the day and night; I feel my days are numbered, and that I must die; and yet I shall die incredulous. As for the moral turpitude that man unveiled to me.'

Lanyon is portrayed as a tortured soul. But, whilst Jekyll's torture has to a certain degree been self-inflicted, it is Jekyll who has accelerated Lanyon's demise. In this passage, Lanyon is clearly plagued by fear and has become deeply unnerved, which is reinforced by the superlative adjective 'deadliest' to describe his 'terror'. Arguably, there's another source of this fear and insecurity. Perhaps Lanyon is not so much

---

[37] Saposnik, p. 723.

frightened by what Jekyll has revealed about himself, but with the hidden self that could surface from within Lanyon. Furthermore, the certainty in the acknowledgement that '[he] must die' suggests that

death may be a better outcome, as it avoids any public revelation of private vice. The graphic imagery of decay and withering in Chapter Six conveys the profound effect that Jekyll has on Lanyon. As flesh covers the skeleton, this withering might also suggest a revelation of what lies beneath the surface. Additionally, the fact that Lanyon's death occurred 'less than a fortnight,' afterwards also indicates how much Jekyll's experiments have traumatized him.

For Lanyon, Hyde becomes 'a cunning tempter [that is] ruthlessly proud of his ability'[38] and perhaps his sudden death is the culmination of what David Punter calls the 'psychic pressures' and 'the strict policing of morality [that came with] [...] Victorian middle-class superiority'.[39]

Structurally, it is also effective that the Lanyon's chapter ends with a focus on Jekyll's 'moral turpitude', as it places the blood of Lanyon's death firmly on Jekyll's hands.

---

[38] Saposnik, p. 724.

[39] David Punter, 'Stevenson, Dr. Jekyll and Mr. Hyde (1886),' in The Gothic, ed. by David Punter and Glennis Byron, (Blackwell Publishing: Oxford, 2004), pp. 226-229 (p. 228).

# Minor characters
## Enfield

Certainly they are an odd pair, aren't they, Enfield and Utterson? Though they are 'distant kinsmen' of some unspecified sort, temperamentally they appear to be almost opposites. While Utterson is an austere, sober-minded lawyer, Enfield is described as a 'well-known man about town'.

What does that phrase suggest about him? Certainly, unlike the other upper-middle class male characters, Enfield is not defined by his work. Whereas Utterson is a lawyer and both Lanyon and Jekyll are doctors, Enfield seems to be defined by his leisure activities, by his pleasures. A 'man-about-town' is like a minor celebrity - a socialite, someone who dresses in natty fashion and likes to be seen at fashionable centres of entertainment – theatres, restaurants and so forth. Sometimes the phrase even carries a slight whiff of the illicit or the notorious about it; a 'man-about-town' can be a bit of a bon-viveur, even a bit of a playboy.

And what, as we asked in our essay on Utterson, are this unlikely pair really doing as they stroll apparently casually through the streets of London in the opening chapter? Certainly there's nothing suspicious about going for a walk together. And why shouldn't two men with very different lifestyles and personalities be close friends? Such friendships exist in the real world, of course. And why too shouldn't two friends value each other's perambulations so much that they put aside everything else so that they can go out together regularly to take the city air?

Perhaps they did just happen to find themselves wandering into the notorious district of Soho. Perhaps they did just happen to find themselves working down a very particular street in Soho. Perhaps everything is just as innocent as it seems.

But, also, particularly in this novella, with its central theme of secrets, facades and misleading appearances, perhaps not.

Are we over-reading here do you think? Acting too much like dogged literary detectives sniffing out hidden clues that are just textual red herrings? Certainly there's something a bit fishy about this attractive Soho street, with a its 'veiled', 'florid charms' and inviting shopfronts displaying their wares like rows of 'smiling saleswomen'. What's being sold here? Then there's the story that Enfield tells of Hyde. If the police had arrived and questioned him, what might Enfield have been willing to tell them about what he was doing out and about at three in the morning? Where precisely was the 'some place' he visited that was 'at the end of the world'? In what sense was this place, which must have been within London, like the 'end of the world'? Possibly there's a perfectly innocent explanation. Or, possibly not.

Even more importantly, though, is how Enfield and Utterson both react to the story. Though he appears to have witnessed a crime – the violent trampling under foot of a young girl, Enfield doesn't seem to even consider reporting this to the police. Perhaps we might expect someone intimately involved with upholding the law to prompt him into doing so. Not a bit of it. Utterson is just as keen to say nothing more about the incident as Enfield.

Possibly, Enfield didn't think the incident serious enough to involve the law. Perhaps. And perhaps not. Soon the odd couple come to the conclusion that a more serious crime might well be taking place, namely blackmail. And, in this case, the blackmail of a fellow Victorian gentleman. With their lives of high public virtue and of private pleasures, some prominent Victorian gentlemen, especially those that Jekyll calls profound 'double-dealers', were particularly prone to and fearful of blackmail. How easily a blackmailer could expose the secret double life and ruin the reputation of an eminent  figure. Call us suspicious, but why are these two respectable citizens with nothing to hide so keen to make a pact to keep secrets and to say nothing?

This is Enfield's explanation:

'You start a question, and it's like starting a stone. You sit quietly on the top of a hill; and away the stone goes, starting others; and presently some bland old bird (the last you would have thought of) is knocked on the head in his own back garden and the family have to change their name. No sir, I make it a rule of mine: the more it looks like Queer Street, the less I ask.'

To which Utterson, a lawyer, responds, 'A very good rule, too'.

Still not convinced that there's something fishy about Mr. Enfield? He appears later on in the novella as a witness to the incident at the window, but then quietly disappears from the narrative. Perhaps he realised that Jekyll could be that 'bland old bird' and his story one that looks far too much like 'Queer Street' for comfort. If Utterson had pursued the truth about Jekyll and Hyde with the dispassionate fervour of the best Victorian detectives, we might not make so much of Enfield's keenness on silence. But put this odd couple together and add Lanyon and Jekyll's secret, private letters and we have something that looks awfully like a conspiracy of silence. A conspiracy of silence

———

designed to protect the public reputations of a small coterie of distinguished and eminent, highly respectable Victorian gentlemen.

## Poole

Though lowly in status, Poole is an important character within the novella. He illuminates the relationship between a Victorian master and his servants and highlights the differences between the classes in the late nineteenth century.

From the outset, Poole is portrayed as a loyal servant to Jekyll. When Utterson questions him about Jekyll's willingness to place 'a great deal of trust' in Hyde, he replies that 'we have all orders to obey him'. It seems that Poole is unwilling to compromise the loyalty that he has forged with Jekyll, and indeed, if a servant at the time dared to challenge the authority of their employers, it could severely damage their chances of future work..

.

Structurally, Stevenson demonstrates that Poole's loyalty towards Jekyll is tested, especially when he sees the extent of his master's experiments. During Chapter Eight, Poole acts takes the decision to visit Utterson, acting decisively of his own accord, despite the potential consequences of this rebounding on him in some unfortunate and damaging way. Though he cannot define it more exactly, Poole insists that 'there is something wrong'. The vague label 'something' signals that whilst he can sense that Jekyll is in danger, as he brands it as 'foul play', he is unable or unwilling to pinpoint it or define it – a pattern that is shared by all the characters in the novella.

We might recall, for instance, Enfield's 'some place'. Poole's decision to visit is certainly brave, as he is deviating from Jekyll's wishes, especially as his master would want his secrets to be kept firmly within the confines of his private cabinet. Here Poole seems to be going beyond what is merely dutiful and acting out of genuine concern for Jekyll's welfare. Perhaps, Stevenson is using Poole to suggest the upper echelons of society have much to learn from those lower in the social hierarchy. It is not materialism or self-interest that dictates Poole's actions, but genuine feelings of concern, anxiety, even pity, emotions which all the Victorian gentleman in the novella seem struggle to express.

 Poole's caring nature towards Jekyll is illustrated when he wishes that he 'may die', as it indicates that he does not want to witness the consequences of Jekyll's experiments. Even though he is consumed with fear, Poole 'doggedly [disregards] the question' that Utterson asks with 'what are you afraid of?' Even Poole suffers from the web of secrecy that Enfield, Utterson, Lanyon and Jekyll weave, admitting that he 'daren't say, sir' what he really suspects. Not only is he genuinely unable to articulate his concerns, but he is also acutely aware of the potential damage to Jekyll's reputation. Clearly, Poole is torn between his duty as a servant to Jekyll and having Jekyll's best interests at heart.

Although the boundaries between master and servant are demonstrated through Jekyll and Poole's relationship, there seems to be a mutual bond between them. Poole may remain passive, which is in keeping and indeed expected of a butler, but he observes the presence in the laboratory, 'that thing', is 'not my master'. The possessive pronoun 'my' signals that he has a close working relationship with Jekyll and illustrates how it is personal to him.

However 'master' establishes the disparity between them in terms of their status - hence the tension between human empathy and duty.

Ultimately, Poole is acutely aware of his position within Jekyll's household. As discussed within the chapter commentaries, Stevenson demonstrates how repressive social conventions can blind characters from seeing or admitting the truth. It seems that the thinking of those in the upper echelons of society is most constrained by such rigidity. As Utterson acknowledges the situation within Jekyll's laboratory is 'beyond' him. In contrast, Poole openly accepts how the surrounding environment 'has seen some strange things', showing him to be willing to embrace the unknown. The implication is that Poole's mind has not been stifled by the oppressive conventions that seem to paralyse and burden Victorian gentleman.

Furthermore, unlike Utterson, Poole is also depicted as a man of action. He is the one that 'swung the axe' and thus broke down one the novella's most significant locked doors, and in doing so exposes the secrets that Jekyll had kept hidden for so long. Here, Poole takes the lead. Utterson is secondary. Stevenson is challenging conventional depictions of the classes, as the upper-middle class lawyer is flummoxed and passive, while Poole acts decisively to reveal the hidden truth.

Stevenson also employs Poole to suggests the potential of bringing unity between the classes. After Poole's visit to Utterson, they work together to solve the final enigma surrounding Jekyll and Hyde. It is, therefore, fitting that Poole and Utterson – men who represent opposing ends of the class spectrum '[lock] the door of the theatre behind them'. This action reflects the shared understanding between. However, whereas Utterson is trapped in a cycle of secrecy that seems to follow him right to the end of the novella, Poole provides hope for the future. Poole's thinking is more flexible - he is willing to accept the unknown and the irrational. Clearly, Stevenson uses Poole to demonstrate that Victorian society had to change and become both less secretive and more open-minded.

# The landlady

If Poole acts as an extension of the benevolent side of Jekyll's nature, it is possible to view Hyde's landlady as a reflection of Hyde's malevolence. Even the idea of duality is evident through the servants in the novella, as both Poole and Hyde's maid are  opposites.

In Chapter Four, the reader is briefly introduced to Hyde's maid. She is described as 'an ivory-faced and silvery-haired old woman' and the compound adjective 'ivory-faced' is effective, as ivory is associated with being solid and hard. This hardness reflects the maid's character – she is as hard and ruthless as Hyde. The reader is never given any indication of the landlady's name; she is simply labelled as 'woman'. Stevenson could be highlighting here how in Victorian England one's class and gender determined the extent to which an one was considered an individual. Her minimal role in this chapter also reflects how those from the lower echelons of society were kept out of the limelight and in the shadows.

Hyde's landlady is described as having 'an evil face, smoothed by hypocrisy, but her manners were excellent.' The adjective used to describe her face is startlingly judgemental and reflects how prone Victorian society was to pass judgements based on appearances. The verb 'smoothed' is also associated with ironing out imperfections, and it is reminiscent description of Jekyll's smoothness. Both Jekyll and the landlady disguise their true selves for the sake of social conventions. Furthermore, the contrast between her 'evil face' and her 'manners [being] excellent' demonstrates that she is another double dealer. Clearly, Hyde's landlady cannot be trusted, in the same manner as Hyde himself.

A lack of trust is exemplified further, as she is very quick to inform Utterson and the Inspector that Hyde's 'habits were very irregular', a frankness about her master quite unlike the loyal  Poole, who 'doggedly disregard[ed] the question' that Utterson asks him. Nevertheless something is being kept secret by the landlady, as she 'declare[d] it was impossible' to 'see [Hyde's] rooms'. The status of Inspector Newcomen is enough to overcome her initial resistance. The fact she does not display much resistance, signals her lack of loyalty towards Hyde, another vast difference to Poole who refuses to pass judgement on his master until the last moment.

'A flash of odious joy' passes over her face. This conveys a rush of excitement and pleasure she gains from this incident. Quick to observe that Hyde 'is in trouble', she probes the Inspector and Utterson with the question 'What has he done?' This presents her perhaps as driven by malicious gossip, though it seems that she may also be trying to gain insights into the secrets of her master. The reasons for this remain inscrutable. Future leverage perhaps, or even material for a potential blackmail.

All in all, the relationship between Hyde and the landlady appears to be the binary opposite to Jekyll's with Poole. While the latter's relationship with his master seems to be based on genuine affection, trust and respect, the landlady's relationship with Hyde is one of short-lived and selfish mutual convenience.

# Themes

## Twinship and disability

Whilst the novella has been viewed as 'a moral allegory, a reflection of colonial and class fears [and] an expression of panic about homosexuality',[40] it is also possible to interpret the Jekyll-Hyde division as a representation of the 'phenomenon of twinship'. Indeed, Stevenson was very much interested in the idea of conjoined twins. In particular, Stevenson was fascinated by the research carried out by Francis Galton, who examined life experiences of twinship.[41]

Before we consider this reading of the novella, it is important to situate it within the context that shaped Stevenson's work. One critic points out that twins were not exactly 'a rare phenomenon in nineteenth century Britain' as 'conjoined twins [...] were a staple of the hugely popular Victorian freak shows that toured the nation.'[42] For instance, Chang and Eng Bunker, were the original Siamese twins and first visited Edinburgh in 1830. Their popularity led to 'their manager [exhausting] his advertising budget [to promote] their appearance.'[43] The idea of twinship also generated numerous debates about whether

---

[40] Emily A. Bernhard Jackson, 'Twins, Twinship, and Robert Louis Stevenson's *The Strange Case of Dr. Jekyll and Mr. Hyde,' Victorian Review*, Spring 2013, Volume. 39, No. 1., (Spring, 2013), pp. 70-86 (p. 70).

[41] Jackson, p. 71.

[42] Jackson, p. 71.

[43] Jackson, p. 71.

conjoined twins were actually 'more than one person'[44] as well the notion of the 'parasite twin'[45] that feeds of the other for survival. Certainly, if we apply these ideas to the portrayal of Hyde, clear connections can be drawn.

From the outset of the novella, Hyde can be seen to embody the

notion of the 'parasite twin'. Entirely dependent on his twin, Hyde simply cannot exist without Jekyll. If Jekyll decides not to take his transformative drug, Hyde cannot spring to life. And as Hyde increases in strength, Jekyll weakens, as if are fed from the same source and the former is draining the life-force from the other.

Victorian society was already 'struggling to define the human and the self in the face of Darwin, crumbling religion, and [...] psychology.'[46] The disturbing questions that twinship posed about human individuality was perhaps too much for society to handle. Even more so, the 'parasite twin' idea is demonstrated further through the reversal of power between Jekyll and Hyde.

As the novella develops, it is Hyde's 'apelike tricks' that get the upper hand, whilst Jekyll acknowledges that he has lost control of his 'original and better self,' thus enabling Hyde to grow 'in stature'.

If we adopt this reading of twinship, Stevenson's portrayal of Jekyll and Hyde's symbiotic relationships reflects the way conjoined twins were

---

[44] Jackson, p. 72.

[45] Jackson, p. 71.

[46] Jackson, p. 72.

regarded in nineteenth century culture. Moreover the idea of the 'parasite twin' gives another model for Hyde's character and his relationship with Jekyll. The focus upon Hyde's abnormal walking as 'stumping', Hyde being 'more of a dwarf' rather than the 'tall fine build of a man' that is Jekyll certainly positions him as the abnormal conjoined twin.

The way that Hyde 'came out roaring' from his 'long caged' existence could be Stevenson delivering a warning against marginalization and persecution. Perhaps, the violent outbreak of Hyde reflects the rage of those treated as outcasts by society, those people who didn't fit Victorian conventions of normality and were labelled as degenerates or freaks. Ultimately, reading this novella from the perspective of twinship helps to emphasise its longevity. The way that Stevenson illuminates how the outsider is treated and the importance of looking beyond the exterior of an individual has more relevance than ever in our current society. As one critic opines:

> 'Faced with a divided self, *Dr. Jekyll and Mr. Hyde* offers the same solution that conjoined and parasite twins wordlessly suggest: that this paradoxically multiple individuality should simply be accepted rather than anatomized. The novella is thus the moral allegory it has always been taken to be, but its moral is both simpler and harder to live with: man is at least two, and at least of those two is less than morally sound.'[47]

---

[47] Jackson, p. 73.

## The Gentleman Question

Although some critics point argue that the novella is predominantly about 'psychological doubling [...] evolution and social ills',[48] the text also explores the notion of the Victorian gentleman, and most importantly, what it in fact means to be a gentleman in the context of the late nineteenth century. As the role of women began to be questioned, because of the 'New Woman,' it triggered questions about masculinity and the position of men in society. Central to this novella then are the two fundamental questions: What makes a gentleman? And are they all that they seem?

Stevenson taps into similar concerns surrounding the 'gentleman question' as other Victorian writers. In Dickens' *Great Expectation*, Pip's desire to remove the label of 'a common labouring boy' so that he can win Estella's heart leads him on a path of self-discovery. Notably, he tries to become a gentleman with the accompanying trappings of material possessions and wealth. Happiness, Pip discovers, is not, however, guaranteed.

Something similar can be said about Jekyll in *The Strange Case*. Born into wealth, Jekyll is a respected scientist and leads a comfortable existence, shielded from the extremes of Victorian poverty. But this is not enough to quench his inner desires. Rather the pressure of maintaining his gentlemanliness increases the potency of his repressed desires. Stevenson demonstrates in this novella the idea that being a Victorian gentleman could cause much discontentment, and all the upper middle-class male characters in the text suffer from the same burdens, whether that be the 'austere' Utterson, the 'man about town'

---

[48] Benjamin D. O'Dell, 'Character Crisis: Hegemonic Negotiations in Robert Louis Stevenson's *Strange Case of Dr. Jekyll and Mr. Hyde*,' in *Victorian Literature and Culture*, 2012, Vol. 40, No. 2 (2012), pp. 509-521 (p. 510).

Enfield or the rational Lanyon.

As in Wilde's *The Picture of Dorian Grey*, the idea of reputation is inextricably linked with the notion of the gentleman. Dorian is advised that 'Every gentleman is interested in his good name. You don't want people to talk of you as something vile and degraded'. Indeed, this parallels the situation of the male characters in Stevenson's novella. They too are preoccupied with maintaining their reputation and fear public disapproval. As Utterson, who should be investigating the 'case' says, it is better 'to say nothing'. Utterson even attempts to silence Mr. Guest, trying to prevent him from speaking about Jekyll's association with Hyde: 'I wouldn't speak of this note, you know'. And like the warning given to Dorian, Jekyll is concerned about what 'this hateful business has rather exposed'.

One critic opines that the notion of the Victorian gentleman was simply 'a mask' and that the gentleman 'used [their] isolation as a [...] tool to generate power.'[49] Preserving the morally upright image of the gentleman came with a high price, as 'maintaining the appearance [of] affluence [...] demand[ed] persistent control and restraint'[50]. What is more, when this 'restraint' could be not be achieved, the gentleman would 'turn inward to the isolation of secret societies, and fraternal organizations, of private studies and their homes'[51] and ultimately meant that the notion of the 'Victorian gentleman [...] [became] the mask of shame'.[52]

---

[49] James Eli Adams in O'Dell, p. 512.

[50] James Eli Adams in O'Dell, p. 512.

[51] James Eli Adams in O'Dell, p. 512.

[52] James Eli Adams in O'Dell, p. 512.

As the novella progresses, Jekyll gradually becomes imprisoned inside the private sphere, as this refuge is the only place where he can grapple with the tensions between the gentlemanly self he wishes to project in public and the private sinner within. Although it is not apparent at first that Jekyll is battling with the 'mask' of respectability, the final chapter illuminates how much he has been at the mercy of social conventions. Initially, whilst the reader may see Jekyll as arrogant and hubristic, this harshness dissolves into some degree of sympathy, as his rationale for utilising science becomes clear: to escape the straight jacket with which Victorian society constrained his psyche. Jekyll labels himself as not being 'in no sense a hypocrite', indicating that he would rather he could split his  civilised and uncivilised self in two so that he can exist freely and without the burdens of being both crushing him.

Jekyll is an exemplar of the Victorian gentleman of the late nineteenth century. Through his character, the reader learns how these powerful  world-shaping men become victim to the social conventions they themselves maintained and regulated. In Chapter Ten, what seems to be a minor burden at the start, enlarges so much as to consume Jekyll: He feels that it is his 'doom' that 'life is bound for ever on man's shoulders and when the attempt is made to cast it off, it but returns upon us with more unfamiliar and more awful pressure.' Here, the plosive 'bound,' alongside the noun phrase 'awful pressure' reflects Stevenson's central concern that these conventions had become intolerable. Their psychological pressure created a schism in the self, leading Victorian men to a double existence, with any escape from the rigidity of being a Victorian gentleman leading them into crime and corruption. The attributive adjective 'awful' that describes 'pressure' is also important, as it intensifies the severity of burdens that Jekyll must carry within himself, and makes the reader recognise his desperation to break free from the straight jacket of convention.

When he first transforms into Hyde, Jekyll feels liberated, replenished and rejuvenated. As Hyde, he can exist outside the conventions expected of a gentleman. As we have seen, one potential reading of Hyde's character is as an embodiment of the marginalised and exploited working-classes. If we adopt this reading, the renewed vigour Jekyll feels as Hyde would suggest the hidden potential power of the working-classes. In addition, though working-class people may have struggled to make ends meet in an era of terrible social deprivation, at least they were not constrained in the ways that Victorian gentleman appeared to be. Though that may not have been much consolation when you lived in slums, worked in factories and didn't have enough to eat. Nor should we ignore the fact that Hyde is demonized in the novella, reflecting the ways the working classes were often viewed by their social superiors.

Stevenson also critiques the notion of Victorian gentlemanliness through the actions of Hyde. Jekyll's desire to unleash the evil within him illustrates that respectability displayed on the surface can be nothing more than artificial, a façade. Perhaps this explains the bestial and brutal attack that Hyde performs upon Sir Danvers Carew. Hyde leaves his victim 'incredibly mangled' – mangling the form of the perfect Victorian gentleman. Furthermore, the 'very tough' cane that 'had broken' with 'one splintered half [...] roll[ing] in the neighbouring gutter' may express Jekyll's violent rejection and rebellion against the conventions of behaviour that entrapped him. In this sense, Stevenson binds the gentleman and the criminal together as one. Indeed, not long after the novella was published, in the real world the Jack the Ripper murders suggested that even the most seemingly civilized members of male Victorian society could also be horrific, brutal killers.

What is more, as Hogle points out, the novella demonstrates that regardless of the conventions in place, Stevenson forces the reader to accept 'the fluidity of potential'[53] and that the individual 'cannot, beat down and deny'[54] what is hidden beneath the surface of a socially constructed self.

Ultimately, Stevenson's novella emphasises then that the title of a 'gentleman' in the late nineteenth century was simply a façade that provided men with the opportunity, as Jekyll puts it, to be 'double-dealers'. As we will indeed see, this notion of the gentleman is also inextricably linked with ideas surrounding sexuality and secrecy.

---

[53] Jerrold E. Hogle, 'Stevenson, Robert Louis (1850-94),' in *The Handbook to Gothic Literature*, ed. by Marie Mulbey Roberts, (Macmillan: Basingstoke, 1998), pp. 220-223 (p. 223).

[54] Hogle, p. 223.

## Homosexuality, Clubland and Secrecy

In July 1889 a fifteen-year-old boy, Charles Swinscow, was questioned in relation to a robbery at the London Central Telegraph office. Though a lowly telegraph-boy, Swinscow had on his person fifteen shillings, the equivalent of many weeks' worth of wages. Under pressure, Swinscow admitted to earning the money through working as a prostitute at a male brothel operating at 19 Cleveland Street. Soon allegations had been made that several eminent, aristocratic Victorians, most notably Lord Arthur Somerset, were among the regular clients of the brothel.

During the subsequent investigation it seems the police were, like Utterson, rather slow to pursue certain lines of inquiry. The eventual trial was also limited in scope and controversial, while the coverage of  the scandal in the press was minimal until it featured in an obscure radical weekly, *The North London Press*. The tensions in Stevenson's novella between revelation and concealment are clearly reflected in the Cleveland Street Scandal, where, though there was a trial, there also appears to have been something of a cover-up.

According to Michel Foucault, 'the late nineteenth century saw an explosion of discourses on sex and sexuality'.[55] Gothic fiction of the period echoes these emerging discourses. One critic points out that in the fin-de-siècle a form of 'silenced homosexuality' was in play, a phenomena increased by the Labouchere Amendment that led to homosexuality

---

[55] Michel Foucault in Antonio Sanna 'Silent Homosexuality in Oscar Wilde's Teleny and The Picture of Dorian Gray and Robert Louis Stevenson's Dr. Jekyll and Mr. Hyde,' *Law and Literature*, Vol. 24, No. 1, Silence (Spring 2012), pp. 21-39 (p. 21).

being branded as 'an unhealthy form of malady'.[56]

Indeed, this idea of silencing is evident in many details of the novella. Though homosexuality is never explicitly mentioned, there are clear clues to its coded presence. Ultimately, the way that homosexuality is never openly acknowledged echoes fears of homosexuality in Late Victorian society.

The novella is almost entirely homosocial; it focuses solely on male characters and the way they interact with each other. Whilst on one level, this could reflect a desire to keep to gender norms and emphasise the patriarchal nature of Victorian society, it also establishes the centrality of relationships exclusively between men. The eminent critic, Elaine Showalter suggests that the male characters are part of a social network that she labels the 'Clubland'. According to Showalter, this functions to provide 'an exclusively male sphere designed to reinforce the solidity of patriarchal values in an era of gendered uncertainty'.[57] She goes on to explain Clubland reveals the 'forbidden emotions between men [within] the dark side of patriarchy.'[58] Jekyll surrounds himself with 'all intelligent reputable men'. What is more, there are subtle hints that the male characters are negotiating the 'dark space' of patriarchy. Enfield reveals to Utterson that he was at 'some place at the end of the world' and notes it was at 'three o'clock'. Meanwhile, Sir Danvers Carew also walked the London streets at night, accosting a young man, Hyde, who beats him to death.

---

[56] Sanna, p. 23.

[57] Benjamin D. O'Dell, 'CHARACTER CRISIS: HEGEMONIC NEGOTIATIONS IN ROBERT LOUIS STEVENSON'S "STRANGE CASE OF DR. JEKYLL AND MR. HYDE", *Victorian Literature and Culture*, 2012, Vol. 40, No. 2 (2012), pp. 509-521 (p. 514).

[58] O'Dell, p. 514.

All of the male characters in the novella can be interpreted to reflect what Antonio Sanna calls 'the silencing of Victorian homosexuals'.[59] Stevenson also highlights the consequences of this silencing: torture and self-destruction. As already established Enfield's actions are already in question, but Utterson is equally conscious of 'his own past' and fears 'some Jack-in-the-Box'. The image is fitting, especially when adopting a queer reading, as it reflects the way Victorian men would subdue their true feelings for the sake of social conventions, and thus avoid disgrace. Utterson also parallels Jekyll in that he despises the 'many ill things he had done' in his youth and is consumed by 'a morbid sense of shame' over the 'profound duplicity of life'. As Sanna point outs, this reflects the period, as 'the fear of exposure, of being talked about in public, and being officially designated as homosexual'[60] was a major anxiety for Victorian gentlemen. It was also a risk that some men had to take in the pursuit of an authentic identity. No wonder then that the idea of secrecy and hushing-up dominates the novella.

 One of the key symbols that reappears throughout the novella is the locked door. The word 'door' appears at least fifty-nine times in the novella, confirming its significance. Of course, a locked door forms a boundary, often in this text between the public and private sphere, and the door enables secrets to be contained within. Structurally, it is noteworthy that at the beginning of the novella, doors remain closed, but, at the end, they are forced open. For instance, in Chapter Nine, when Poole 'swung the axe' it causesa 'blow [that] shook the building'.

---

[59] Sanna, p. 24.

[60] Sanna, p. 24.

Another critic states that, *'Fin-de-siècle* images of forced penetration through locked doors into private cabinets, rooms and closets permeate Utterson's narrative'.[61] Stephen Heath adds that 'the organising image' for Stevenson's narrative 'is the breaking down of doors, learning the secret behind them'.[62]

If we continue to apply a queer reading to the novella, Hyde is positioned as a tempting as well as repulsive force. All the characters feel immense hatred towards him, yet they cannot detach themselves from him. This reflects feelings and attitudes towards homosexuality at the time. The semantic field conveying reactions to Hyde - 'unspeakable', 'displeasing,' 'detestable,' 'unknown disgust', 'loathing' – expresses the prejudice towards those who did not align to conventional heteronormative relationships. As Sanna notes, the 'pleasures [in the novella] are seen as undignified because society considers them as such, not because they are vicious in themselves'.[63] Moreover, this negative depiction of Hyde reflects 'the cultural figuration of homosexuality as "monstrous" [...] [and] is symptomatic of both [...] attraction toward and repudiation of this dangerous figure of desire'.[64]

---

[61] Elaine Showalter, 'Dr. Jekyll's Closest,' in *Sexual Anarchy: Gender and Culture at the Fin de Siècle.* (New York: Viking), p. 6.

[62] Heath, "Psychopathia sexualis," in Elaine Showalter, 'Dr. Jekyll's Closest,' in *Sexual Anarchy: Gender and Culture at the Fin de Siècle.* (New York: Viking), p. 6.

[63] Sanna, p. 26.

[64] Kelly Hurley, 'British Gothic Fiction, 1885-1930,' in *The Cambridge Companion to Gothic fiction,* ed. by Jerrold E. Hogle, (Cambridge: Cambridge University Press, p. 2002), pp. 189-207) (p. 199).

Finally, in the novella, we also see that Jekyll is a conflicted soul Again, this reflects the 'silenced homosexual' who would carry the burden of their secret identity for the sake of their survival in a repressive society. It is, therefore, significant that Hyde is 'younger, lighter, happier' as it signals that Jekyll can only throw off propriety and express his desires without constraint as Hyde. In contrast, Jekyll admits that he his conventional life is an 'unhappy' one. This reflects Stevenson's concerns about repressive attitudes towards sexuality and the consequences of 'otherising'. Only in death can Jekyll escape living in fear of his 'devil' that was once 'long caged' but now can break free. As Sanna accurately concludes:

> 'Jekyll's life is not portrayed as happily as Hyde's. The repression of a person's sexuality is considered extremely detrimental to the individual, whereas the ability to freely experience natural urges and pleasures leads to happiness and serenity.'[65]

---

[65] Sanna, p. 27.

## Father and Son

Although the novella has been predominantly seen as a reflection of the *fin-de-siècle* fears surrounding 'national, social and psychic decay',[66] it is also possible to interpret the relationship between Jekyll and Hyde as a mirror image of Stevenson's with his own father. Whilst the idea is only briefly hinted at in the novella with Jekyll taking 'a father's interest' in Hyde, it is evident that Hyde adopts the role of a son who needs guidance but who also relished the opportunity to exist freely.

It is well documented by critics that Stevenson's relationship with his father was an extremely conflicted one. As one critic notes, 'Stevenson's relations with his family, especially his father, produced deep tensions and guilts throughout his life'.[67] Indeed we see such tensions reflected in the novella. From the outset, Hyde is portrayed as like a child. He is described as 'stumping along' and several characters comment on how he is 'dressed in clothes far too large for him', an image that might suggest the father's influence swamps his child. In Chapter Ten Jekyll notes that Hyde was 'smaller, lighter, and younger,' positioning him as the son, with a new lease of life. Later Jekyll notes that 'Hyde had grown in stature' reflecting the idea of growth of a child. In the final chapter, Jekyll also seems to have aged, referring to himself as 'elderly', thus emphasizing the apparent age difference between him and Hyde. Perhaps, Stevenson is suggesting that such tensions can be avoided, unless the father accepts that the child must exist freely and independently.

---

[66] Douglas Gifford, 'The Importance of *The Master of Ballantrae*,' in *Robert Louis Stevenson: Bloom's Modern Critical Views*, ed. by Harold Bloom, (Chelsea House Publishers: USA, 2005), pp. 53-78 (p. 61).

[67] Gifford, p. 62.

When this is not accepted, greater conflict will follow.

If we adopt the reading of Jekyll and Hyde mirroring Stevenson's strained relationship with his father, then the aggression that Hyde demonstrates is perhaps an expression of intergenerational angst.

Perhaps leaving Sir Danvers Carew – that model Victorian gentleman – as 'incredibly mangled' expresses a hostility to father figures, father figures who have created the stifling, claustrophobic conditions of Victorian culture. Such angst is evident in Stevenson's letters. In one he desires his father to take him 'as you find me', but realises that as a son he is 'a subject for scolding', a word that infantilises the writers. Elsewhere in his letters Stevenson also expresses frustrations that resonate with his characters of Jekyll and Hyde: 'Daily life is one repression', he writes, 'from beginning to end'.[68]

Jekyll's declaration that he 'cannot say [that] care[s] what becomes of Hyde [and he is] quite alone with him' reflects the idea of disowning a child through shame. Like Victor Frankenstein, in creating a new life, Jekyll usurps the roles of both the mother figure and of God. Like Victor Frankenstein, Jekyll is horrified by his monstrous progeny and like Victor he rejects and abandons his creation. However, appalled by the ugliness of the creature he has created, Victor immediately rejects and abandons it. In contrast, initially Jekyll indulges Hyde, gives him his liberty and then is shocked into rejection when Hyde's appetites become dissolute and depraved.

[68] Robert Louis Stevenson in William Gray's 'The English Scene,' in *Robert Louis Stevenson: A Literary Life*, (Palgrave: Basingstoke, 2004), pp. 1-22 (p. 7).

Jekyll's acknowledgement that he has 'lost confidence in [himself]' could illustrate the consequences of a strained relationship between a father and son, perhaps even a father's despair at how his son has turned out. Whilst one reading positions the Jekyll/Hyde relationship as emblematic of the nineteenth century drug addict, his eagerness to detach himself from Hyde, and how instantly this rebounds on him could reflect the tug-of-war nature of relationships between fathers and sons. Stevenson may also be suggesting that it is not always possible to completely break free from parental bonds, regardless of how overwhelming or toxic they may be. After all Jekyll and Hyde are dependent on each other, their relationship is symbiotic, as they both perish at the end. [Though, as we suggested in our discussion of twins, it can also be read as parasitic.]

Stevenson's letters enable us to make further connections to the father-son relationship that is at play in the novella. Stevenson labels himself as 'an egotistical brute'[69] and this is reminiscent of what Jekyll says about the darker side of his nature: 'I still hated the brute that slept within me.' Perhaps, Stevenson uses Hyde to reflect how he feels his own father perceived him.

Alternatively, Hyde may also symbolise what Stevenson craved: the opportunity to break free from his repressed existence so that he was free to express his feelings and form his own authentic identity, which is something that he could not do with the shadow of his father overhanging him. If we extend this reading further then, perhaps the way Hyde takes pleasure in 'destroying the portrait of [his] father' reflects Stevenson's own desire to erase his father's overshadowing

---

[69] William Veeder, 'Children of the Night: Stevenson and Patriarchy,' in *Robert Louis Stevenson: Bloom's Modern Critical Views*, , ed. by Harold Bloom, (Chelsea House Publishers: USA, 2005), pp. 103-158 (p. 111).

influence.

Structurally, the reader sees how suffocating such relationships can become. At the beginning of the novella, Jekyll is confident that he can 'be rid of Hyde' whenever he chooses, yet in Chapter Ten, he acknowledges that he 'fell in slavery'. This may reflect the possible parental fears, with the father losing the ability to control and dictate the development of their own flesh and blood. As well, the way he had 'gone to bed [as] Henry Jekyll' yet 'awakened [as] Edward Hyde' is also significant, as it conveys the idea that within such a strained familial relationship, it is inevitable for the repressed to break free.

Overall, as one critic succinctly points out, Stevenson's novella is so effective as he 'transforms biographical materials and emotions into a critical portrait of his times' and in doing so, the reader is provided with snapshots of the writer's own inner tensions and conflicts. Altogether then, Stevenson is clearly depicting the relationship between father and son as suffocating. He also emphasises that such bonds can only be healthy when there is mutual love and warmth exchanged, as well as when there is an acceptance by the parent figure that the child will always desire to forge their own path. If this independence is not granted, the consequences can be catastrophic.

## Darwinism and Degeneration

As already noted in the chapter commentaries, the *fin-de-siècle* was a period of enormous turbulence and anxiety. One of the key concerns  that fuelled such fears the theory of evolution. It triggered the central concern that if a species has the potential to move upwards through the evolutionary chain, could it possibly revert downwards. Stevenson's *The Strange Case* clearly engages with such discourses about reverse evolution or what came to be called degeneration. Before we consider how Stevenson engages with the idea of degeneration in his novella, it is important to understand the context. According to Kelly Hurley, Darwinian science had 'destabilising effects' on Late Victorian culture as the theory of evolution outlined how all animal species were 'impermanent, metamorphic, and liable to extinction.'[70]

The theory of evolution also seemed to undermine Christianity, particularly in terms of an explanation of the beginnings of life. Rather than the world being created as it is by God, perhaps only a few thousand years ago, Darwin showed how evolution was an ongoing radically transformative process that operated over far, far greater periods of time. Moreover, his theory showed that humans were not separate or outside of this process but, in fact, were part of the animal kingdom, having evolved from apes.

---

[70] Kelly Hurley, 'British Gothic Fiction, 1885-1930,' in *The Cambridge Companion to Gothic Fiction*, ed. by Jerrold E. Hogle, (Cambridge: Cambridge University Press, 2002), pp. 189-207 (p. 195).

In *The Descent of Man* (1871) Darwin made explicit the implications of evolutionary theory - that humans had 'descended from a hairy, tailed quadruped'.[71] Stevenson gives Hyde ape-like features. Jekyll recalls his hand, for example was 'corded and hairy'. Indeed the phrase 'ape-like' is used specifically about Hyde when he attacks Sir Danvers Carew. Ultimately, as Hurley emphasises, to Victorian readers Darwin's work seemed to portray 'the human body [...] as a kind of Frankenstein monster, patched together from the different animal forms the human species had inhabited during the various phases of its evolutionary history'.[72] Such ideas permeate late nineteenth century discourses. For example Bram Stoker creates the shapeshifting Count Dracula and H. G. Wells uses both the Morlocks in *The Time Machine* and the abhumans [creatures that are part human and part animal] in *The Island of Dr. Moreau* to explore similar concerns.

Throughout Stevenson's novella, a semantic field of animalistic traits is used to describe Hyde. He makes 'a hissing intake of breath'; he 'snarled'; he is 'a pale and dwarfish'. Moreover, he has 'ape-like traits' and his 'ape-like spite' is aimed at the supposedly civilised Jekyll. All these references position Hyde as half-human, half-animal – as an abhuman figure. Clearly referencing degeneration theory, Stevenson also describes him as like a caveman or a neanderthal, as 'troglodytic'. While it is no surprise that all the other characters express fear about and hatred towards Hyde, their reaction to him shows that supposedly civilized characters can also become violently animalistic in certain circumstances.

---

[71] Charles Darwin in Kelly Hurley, 'British Gothic Fiction, 1885-1930,' in *The Cambridge Companion to Gothic Fiction*, ed. by Jerrold E. Hogle, (Cambridge: Cambridge University Press, 2002), pp. 189-207 (p. 195).

[72] Hurley, p. 195.

Alongside this, Stevenson's novella uses the character of Hyde to warn against complacency about the human condition and presents similar concerns to those explored by H.G. Wells. For instance, in Wells' novella, *The Time Machine,* the narrator visits future time and finds that all humanity has been split in two separate species, the Eloi and the Morlocks. The Morlocks, who are bestial degenerates, prey upon the effete Eloi. As one critic points out, such texts caution 'against the complacent assumption [of] humanity's upward progression [on] the evolutionary scale'.[73]

If we adopt a Darwinian reading of the novella, the way that Jekyll loses control and becomes dominated by the degenerate Hyde expresses fears that a new race of degenerate humans might, in time, topple civilization and destroy humanity as we know it. The way that Edward Hyde grows in 'stature' as the novella progresses, while Jekyll seems to become older and weaker, reflects another Darwinian notion, that of 'The Survival of the Fittest'. The evolutionary process is a battle in which life-forms best adapted to their environment survive. If the whole of London becomes like the worst of Victorian slums, then that environment will favour the Hydes over the Jekylls.

Nicholas Ruddick argues that there was a very real fear during the fin-de-siècle that 'human beings might revert atavistically to ancestral forms under the unprecedented stresses of modern life' and a widespread anxiety that 'a 'savage,' 'ape,' or 'beast' was latent in

73 Steven McLean, 'Heart of Darkness: *The Time Machine* and Retrogression' in *The Early Fiction of H.G. Wells: Fantasies of Science* (New York: Palgrave Macmillan, 2009) pp. 11-40 (p. 32).

everyone' and, moreover was 'threatening to get loose'.[74]

These fears are exemplified in Stevenson's novella as Hyde is constantly aligned with the bestial and savage, but Stevenson also offers subtle hints that Hyde's degenerate traits were an integral part of Jekyll long before Hyde was released. It is one thing to assume, as many degeneration theorists did, that a race of monstrous, degenerate humans might be bred by Victorian urban squalor and quite another to suggest that this degeneracy might be both contained within civilised gentleman and that the repression of this inner animal might turn this inner animal into a savage beast or a monster.

As Ruddick also notes, 'the aftermath of the Darwinian revolution' led to 'humanity's place in biological nature [and] evolutionary time'[75] being questioned. Overall, Stevenson's novella clearly engages with the fears surrounding evolution and its reverse, degeneration. Whilst Wells' *The Time Machine* ends on a pessimistic note, with humanity consumed by its own animalistic progeny, Stevenson warns us through the role reversal of Jekyll and Hyde that humankind, and the civilization we have built, is no more stable than any other life form and that if we can go progress forwards, in certain conditions, we might also be in danger of regressing and slipping back towards the mire.

---

[74] Nicholas Ruddick, 'The fantastic fiction of the fin de siècle,' in *The Cambridge Companion to The Fin de Siècle,* ed. by Gail Marshall, (Cambridge: Cambridge University Press, 2007), pp. 189-206 (p. 190-191).

[75] Ruddick, pp. 204-205.

## Drugs and addiction

Throughout the novella, Stevenson explores the idea of addiction, reflecting the wider concerns surrounding drug consumption at the end of the nineteenth century. Beneath the polite façade of respectable upper-middle class society, drug addiction was becoming an increasing problem. Drugs seemed to offer an escape from the straight jacket of social conventions of the era. In this sense, Jekyll is an emblem of the nineteenth century drug addict, taking his 'potion' to liberate himself and to seek pleasure. Equally, Hyde is also an emblem of addiction, as he is despised by those that encounter him, but nevertheless, they are attracted towards him.

According to Patricia Comitini, addiction became a pressing issue during the *fin-de-siècle*. She notes that those that theorised about addiction felt that it marked 'a debased moral nature'.[76] Certainly Jekyll's use of drugs unleashes the worst within him. Drugs are, also, of course, the source of his demise. Victorian medic, J.B. Mattison, viewed addiction 'among medical men as an inestimable problem that threatens to undo the profession'.[77] Perhaps this explains why Lanyon detaches himself from Jekyll – he recognizes his erstwhile friend as an addict. Another modern critic points out there was a 'steep rise in the number of morphine-addicted doctors during the latter half of the

---

[76] Patricia Comitini, 'The Strange Case of Addiction in Robert Louis Stevenson's "Strange Case of Dr. Jekyll and Mr. Hyde" *Victorian Review*, Spring 2012, Vol. 38, No. 1 (Spring 2012), pp. 113-131 (p. 122).

[77] Comitini, p. 123.

nineteenth century'[78] and Stevenson is perhaps demonstrating that even the most respectable of figures within the profession can fall victim to addiction.

And we can connect this to a crisis trust reflected in the novella. Where might we look as a society for figures we can trust to guide and advise during times of adversity? We might hope that the political classes will be dependable. But we might also look to religious leaders and to our professional classes for reassurance and guidance. Notably, though religious thinking is applied to Hyde as a way to try to understand him – he is variously described as a 'dark soul', a 'devil' and as the 'spirit of hell' – there are no religious characters in Stevenson's novella on hand to help exorcise him from Jekyll. Moreover, the professional classes presented - the lawyers, scientists and doctors are portrayed -  as deeply flawed and unreliable. Clearly this reflects anxieties in Late Victorian culture.

Structurally, the novella charts the consequences of addiction upon the individual. Initially Jekyll is confident that he can be 'rid of Hyde' as and when he chooses, yet the way Hyde overwhelms and takes control demonstrates the struggles involved when having to break free from drug addiction. Later, appalled, Jekyll confesses that he 'had gone to bed [...] [but] awakened [as] Edward Hyde'.

The intensity of Jekyll's addiction is highlighted in Chapter Eight. Poole describes how he was 'crying night and day for some sort of medicine and cannot get it to his mind'. Here, the present participle verb 'crying' alongside 'night' and 'day' conveys the terrible grip of drug addiction.

---

[78] Barry Milligan, 'Morphine-Addicted Doctors, the English Opium-Eater, and Embattled Medical Authority,' *Victorian Literature and Culture*, Vol. 33, No. 2 (2005), pp. 541-553 (p. 541).

Jekyll is deadlocked into a cycle of constant addiction and he is clearly being consumed by the very thing that he thought would bring him pleasure. Combined with 'crying', Poole's description of hearing Jekyll 'weeping like a woman or a lost soul' could also convey the unbearable pains of cold turkey. Indeed, this is highlighted even more so when Poole notes that the 'drug is wanted bitter bad [...] whatever for'.

The physical ravages of drug addiction could also be reflected in Jekyll's deterioration in stature; he shrinks from being a 'tall fine build of a man' to a hunched 'dwarf'.

Ultimately, Stevenson is demonstrating that even the supposedly staunch and reliable Victorian gentleman could fall foul to drug addiction. Drugs, such as opium and cocaine, were rarely taken by working-class members of society. One critic points out, however, that opium addiction within the working-class may have been ignored and that it only became acknowledged as a problem when the middle-classes become addicts.[79] Therefore, the idea of addiction exposes a further issue within Victorian society then: hypocrisy.

Overall, as one critic notes, Victorian society was concerned with excluding 'enemies, pretenders, competitors, corruptions'.[80] Typically these threats were identified as 'women, the working class, foreigners, and criminals'. However, Stevenson challenges such perceptions through Jekyll, as he demonstrates how 'enemies, pretenders, competitors [and] corrupters'[81] can exist within the establishment itself.

---

[79] Livia Gershon, 'How Opium Use Became a Moral Issue,' *JSTOR Daily*, accessed at: https://daily.jstor.org/how-opium-use-became-a-moral-issue/.

[80] Comitini, p. 124.

[81] Comitini, p. 124.

Altogether then, the idea of addiction illuminates Stevenson's concern that Victorian society was founded upon pretences and lies.

It is, therefore, fitting to conclude this chapter with Irving S. Saposnik's assessment of the Jekyll/Hyde dichotomy in the novella:

> 'If Jekyll's fears are taken as a barometer of Victorian anxieties, then his relationship to Hyde becomes apparent. While Jekyll represents a man "in the pink of the proprieties," Hyde is the brutal embodiment of the moral, social, political, and economic threats which shook the uncertain Victorian world.'[82]

---

[82] Irving S. Saposnik, 'The Anatomy of Dr. Jekyll and Mr. Hyde,' Studies in English Literature, 1500-1900 , Autumn, 1971, Vol. 11, No. 4, Nineteenth Century (Autumn, 1971), pp. 715-731 (p. 729).

# Glossary of Terms

Allegory - a narrative with two meanings, an obvious surface one and a more subtle second meaning. For example, George Orwell's *Animal Farm* tells the story of animals rebelling against a tyrannical farmer. The animals' story is a political allegory about the rise of communism

Allusion - A reference to another work of literature.

Analepsis - another term for a flashback

Antagonist - the main opponent of the central character

Byronic Hero - a fascinating, moody Romantic figure, usually rebellious and solitary

Characterisation - the methods used to create characters, such as visual description, interior monologue, through dialogue and so forth

Connotations - the implied meanings and associations of words

Degeneration – evolution reversed

Dramatic Irony - when the audience know information of which the characters are unaware

Epistolary - a novel written in the form of letters

Epithet - an adjective or adjectival phrase that sticks like glue to a character.

Exposition - the setting of the scene and characters in a novel or play

Figurative language - metaphor, simile, symbol and personification

Focalisation - the management of point of view

Foregrounding - bringing something to the reader's attention

Foreshadowing – using ominous details to suggest future disaster

Frame Narrative - a story that surrounds another and gives it context

Free Indirect Discourse - a narrative device in which the author and character's perspectives merge; the author adopting the point of view and/or language of a character

Freudian – influenced by the psychological theories of Sigmund Freud

Imagery - descriptive language that is either figurative or sensory (appeals to the senses)

In Media Res - a Latin term, meaning beginning in the middle of the story

Interior Monologue - the thoughts of a character

Intertextuality - the idea that all texts are connected to and composites of other texts

Intrusive Narrator - a narrator who explicitly enters into the text to comment on characters and/or action

Juxtaposition - when contrasting ideas are placed together

Liminality – a state of inbetweenness, when something is neither quite one thing nor another.

Metonymy - where a concrete attribute of a thing stands in for it. For example, the crown for the monarchy

Mode - the style, manner or method with which the subject is treated

Monologue - a speech in the voice of a single character

Motif - a recurrent pattern of character, image, device, action or emotion in a work of literature

Narrative Structure - the way in which the chronological story has been rearranged by the author. For example, in *Frankenstein* the same story is told first by *Frankenstein* and then by his creation, allowing us to compare their versions.

Omniscient Narrator - a narrator who has a God-like perspective on characters and action

Pathetic Fallacy - the use of nature to symbolise characters' feelings

Picaresque - a narrative that chronicles the misadventures of a likeable rogue

Plosive Alliteration - repetition of p,b, t and d sounds

Prolepsis - another term for a flashforward

Sibilance - the repetition of s sounds

Subtext - the meaning that lies beneath the surface of words

Symbol - a metaphor that has become universally decipherable

Syntax - the order of words in a sentence

Vernacular - the ordinary language of a place or country

# Recommended reading

Bloom, H. [2005] *Robert Louis Stevenson: Bloom's Modern Critical Views*. Chelsea House.

Botting, F. [1996] *Gothic*. Routledge.

Fielding, P. [2020] *The Edinburgh Companion to Robert Louis Stevenson*. Edinburgh University Press.

Heiland, D. [2004] *Gothic and Gender: An Introduction*. Blackwell.

Hogle, J. [2002] *The Cambridge Companion to Gothic Fiction*. CUP.

Marshall, G. [2007] *The Cambridge Companion to the Fin de Siecle*. CUP.

Punter, D. & Byron, G. [2004] *The Gothic*. Blackwell publishing.

Punter, D. [1996] *The Literature of Terror: a History of Gothic Fiction from 1765 to the Present Day*. Longman.

Punter, D. [2000] *A Companion to the Gothic*. Blackwell publishing.

Reid, J. [2006] *Robert Louis Stevenson, Science and the Fin de Siecle*. Macmillan.

Roberts, M. [1998] *The Handbook to Gothic Literature*, Macmillan.

Smith, A. [2007] *Gothic Literature: Edinburgh Critical Guides*. Edinburgh University Press.

# About the authors

Head of English and freelance writer, Neil Bowen has a master's degree in Literature & Education from the University of Cambridge and is a member of Ofqual's experts panel for English. He is the author many books in the 'Art of...' series, including ones on poetry, drama and the novel. Neil runs the peripeteia project, bridging the gap between A-level and degree level English courses **www.peripeteia.webs.com, runs CPD sessions for English teachers and regularly** delivers talks at GCSE & A-level student conferences for The Training Partnership. He tweets at @neilbowen3.

Passionate about trying new Teaching and Learning initiatives, Matthew Moore has taught English for around twelve years. Having completed a Masters in English Literature on dystopian fiction, currently he is pursuing a PhD in English Literature exploring ecocriticism in relation to the fiction of H.G. Wells.

Lightning Source UK Ltd.
Milton Keynes UK
UKHW020122060821
388387UK00006B/1477